Phobias Explained & Script
Pre-talk & Hypnosis
Psychotherapy
& Hypnotherapy
Neuro-Linguistic Programming (NLP)
Cognitive Behavioural Therapy (CBT)
Clinical Psychology

By
David Glenn

I am dedicating this book to my clients, in appreciation.
Thank you, because without you I would never have had the experience,
and therefore the knowledge, to write this book.
David Glenn.

Disclaimer, Legal Warning and Notice

The CD Rom that is mentioned in this book is given to those studying as a Diploma with me personally. It is not given out for free with this book.
☐

Contents

Introduction

THOSE STUDENTS THAT HAVE READ MY BOOK: "Beginner to Advanced Practitioner Training Course & Self Development in Psychotherapy - Hypnotherapy - Neuro-Linguistic Programming (NLP) - Cognitive Behavioural Therapy (CBT)

Clinical Psychology Volume One", will not need to read this book. The information within this book has already been covered in the book just mentioned. Even so, I have also published this script as a separate digital book for those people that requested me to do so.

This book is more than just a phobia script. I will explain what a phobia is, how to overcome the fear, and I will also give many examples of real clients that I treated in therapy. I will show you how I structure a set plan for a phobia therapy session, and of what needs to be done to help the client overcome their problem. Also I will explain to you the knowledge that the client needs to be educated on, in order to help them further. Even though I have a set plan, please remember to always personalise a session to the client within the plan.

The script in this book has been written in a way, not intended to be read out to the clients, word for word. I simply want to show you different beginners and advanced ways of conducting therapy, in a structured session that you can personalise to each client. This script can be adapted and used for any phobia or fear, but as an example I have used spiders. I have written both the pre-talk and what is said under hypnosis to the client far longer than it need be. I have done this purposely, to give you more examples of what can be said, so that you can pick and choose what you feel fits that particular client best. So, once again, please note that this script is not intended to be read word for word to the client. It can even be used in a number of sessions, if needed, to make each session different from the previous.

I am David Glenn, a Professional Psychotherapist, Hypnotherapist, NLP Practitioner and Trainer with over twenty year's experience in this profession. I have written this book to pass on my knowledge for those:

1) Interested in the cognitive psychology of oneself as a self-development help guide in understanding and utilising the power of your own mind to overcome: Fear and Phobias, in order to get the best out of your life.

2) Wanting to have a successful career in Hypnotherapy, Neuro-Linguistic Programming (NLP), Cognitive Behavioural Therapy (CBT), Life Coaching and Psychotherapy as a whole. Developing or enhancing your therapy skills in dealing with phobia clients, to help them recover their cognitive health and wellbeing.

Everybody can study this phobia script course book as home study training. It is laid out in layman's terms, so those with no previous knowledge of the subject, can still learn how to use the power of your own mind to enrich your life. Even if you do not want to be a Professional Therapist, you can still study this course to understand yourself more, for self-help and personal development. This will enable you to break negative habits, and have unlimited confidence with the techniques that you can learn and use in your life, or therapy practice to improve your psyche, or that of a client's cognitive health (psychological health) and wellbeing. You will also learn how to hypnotise your clients, friends and family, and find the beneficial power of self-hypnosis.

Enrich your knowledge and skills with what I am going to teach you, which can be used in general life, for yourself and others, or by those wishing a new profession in Hypnotherapy, CBT, NLP Practitioner or Psychotherapist. Keep an open mind to new possibilities. How you have thought, communicated, and acted throughout life, may need to change, or be adapted for positive effect. I will teach you the tools of how this can be done to enable you or others to move on positively in life.

Once you have read and fully understood this book, for many people it is a life changing experience. My philosophy on therapy and psychology in general is - it is the art of understanding the psychology of people, our behaviour, the mind model, body language, communication and speech. You will be able to understand how your mind works, and how to utilise its power for positive change.

☐

Anyone on earth, if able bodied, can drive, or learn to drive a car. Be that as it may, that does not mean you will ever be a professional rally, or formula one racing car driver. In order to be the formula one expert in the psychotherapy world, you have to have that special something: innate quality. You cannot think, act, or communicate as the general public do. In general life, what you think is rude, morally wrong, or what you would not dream of saying to a fellow human being in public, those same rules do not apply in the therapy room, because the client is paying you for a highly skilled service. You must never allow your own personality to effect what needs to be done, in order to help the client progress forwards positively in their lives. Conducting therapy is not about you or your beliefs; it is about what is best for the client, even if you have to be cruel to be kind, and go outside of your comfort zone. You may have thought that therapy is just about counselling, empathy, listening, understanding, relating to, comforting and simply relaxing a person. It is far more complex than that. You are not there to comfort a client; you are there to enable them to become unstuck, get out from their negative mindset, and move forward for positive effect and self-fulfilment. You are there to enable them to see the wood from the trees, so they can find the truth about themselves. Thereby you can support them with education, by imparting psychotherapy knowledge that can be adapted, to enable growth and movement. You will understand this more as you learn, by reading through this book in full.

I have met many students that have all the knowledge they require to be great Hypnotherapist, CBT, NLP Therapists, but yet many lack intuition. This is a skill that you either already have, or you have not. Without it, success as a psychotherapist will be limited. Of course I have also met many students that have no confidence whatsoever, and I watch them grow and develop into great therapists through the knowledge from my training.

I have a very modern approach to therapy for today's generation, as I am sure you will come to realise as we continue. Once you have absorbed all the knowledge I am about to teach you, you will know more than most therapists that have been in the profession for many years. This book contains valuable information on becoming a Professional Hypnotherapist, and Psychotherapist, despite that I still advise all my students to practise on volunteers, for charities, family and friends, before their first paying client. Conducting psychotherapy is an extremely complex and skilful job. Therefore after reading this book, and gaining some practical skills, if you do not feel you have the ability to put in place the knowledge I have imparted in this book, then I will teach you the skills in a group or one on one setting. Through tailor-made training this will enable you to set up in business, with the greatest confidence in knowledge and skills to succeed in a successful psychotherapy career.

Prepare yourself for a truly amazing, life-changing experience. Enjoy as you learn, and I guarantee, at times you will be thinking: WOW! MIND BLOWING, INSPIRATIONAL KNOWLEDGE AND WISDOM, ALL IN THIS BOOK!

My recommendation is to read this book, in its entirety, more than once, to fully understand the connection between each skill being taught. Please do not speed read this book, or skip chapters. Take your time to absorb all the information being taught.

It will also be most beneficial to put the knowledge and skills into practise, by attending my group training workshop sessions or one to one training.

The Workings of the Mind Model Bulletin Points

AS A STUDENT, before you conduct a therapy session with any type of client, you first must learn the mind model and memorise it. I have added the bulletin points of the Mind Model in this chapter to help you.

Three parts of the whole mind:

1) Conscious Mind Functions: Rational logical thought - Makes decisions, but the subconscious determines on whether those decisions are carried out or not - One task at once - Willpower - General speech.

2) Subconscious Mind Functions: Many tasks at once - Memories - Imagination - Emotions - Habits - Protects us - In control - Intelligence - Perception of reality - Habitual speech.

3) Analytical or Critical Area: This part of the mind is the conduit connection between the conscious and subconscious, passing information between the two main parts of the whole mind. It is the part of the mind that reasons to determine new information as being

fact or fiction (real or fake), based on information from the subconscious memories.

The subconscious four reference points:

(A) The subconscious mind does not know the difference between what is real or imagined.

(B) The subconscious also does not know the difference between good habits, or bad habits. A habit is a habit through repetition regardless.

(C) The subconscious has no concept of time, past, present or future with regards to associated links.

(D) The subconscious also works via associated links, which are memories, cognitive thought (a persons perception of fact or fiction, real or fake, true or false-truth), and emotions (pain or pleasure), that are associated (connected), within the mind to an anchor. This can be any sound, touch, taste, smell, or seeing a certain person (or behaviour), colour, object or place.

The seven mind rules:

1) Ideas or thoughts result in physical immediate emotional reactions.
2) The subconscious mind delivers what we focus on.
3) Repeated negative or positive focused thoughts result in long-term organic change over time.
4) Imagination overpowers knowledge within in the mind.
5) Fixed thoughts can only be replaced by another via the subconscious.
6) Opposing ideas cannot be held at the same time.
7) Conscious effort alone, results in opposite subconscious success.

Seven Important Mind Rules

MOST PEOPLE WRONGLY BELIEVE that the mind and body are two separate things, but the brain is part of the body as a whole, and the mind is part of the brain. You are one being, so the mind and body are the same whole, because they are connected.

One: Ideas or thoughts result in physical immediate emotional reactions - Thought processes affect the reactions of your immediate behaviour, even if you are not consciously aware of your reaction. For example, a micro-signal in the facial area of looking upset. Negative thoughts of any kind develop instantly into negative, physical, emotional changes within the body. Example: blushing, or imagining being upset, or crying in a certain situation, will result in you doing so, by just the thought of being confronted by that situation. If you imagine a spider is going to hurt you, then the imagined idea causes a physical, emotional, negative reaction to fear, even though the spider is of no danger to you and may not even be there. Thoughts that release powerful emotions, whether real or imagined will, without fail, seep into subconscious mind. Physical, emotional reactions then occur, due to the subconscious accepting the negative thoughts as fact. This is due to the subconscious mind not knowing the difference between what is real or imagined. Of course happy thoughts also have an instant effect on your emotions, and therefore your body as well, by having a positive effect on the body unlike negative thoughts. Consider the mind and body as being the same thing, because the mind is part of the body, therefore whatever thought you have, affects every living cell within your body, either negatively or positively, depending on your thought, so it's best to think positively.

Two: The subconscious mind delivers what we focus on - When wanting to achieve a realistic goal that you are not already doing, if you focus your subconscious mind on a negative, then a negative result is what will be achieved and the goal is failed. Alternatively, by playing a positive movie of achieving that same goal within your imagination, then you will achieve that goal on a conscious level, because your subconscious mind believes you have already achieved it, and that makes it easier to do so via the subconscious auto pilot. The reason the subconscious believes you have already achieved the goal, is because you played the positive movie of doing so, and the subconscious mind does not know the difference between what is real or imagined, because both are your reality. You made a conscious decision to do something, your subconscious then plays a positive movie of what you consciously want to achieve, and by doing so, it makes a task easier to achieve, due to the two parts of the mind working in agreement, instead of being in conflict.

What I have just written above, is in relation to a person that wants to achieve a goal that they should be doing, but are not doing it. However, a person with a bad habit is the opposite, because they are already doing something that they should not be doing, so the focus of the subconscious mind has to be different. A person with a bad habit wrongly focuses the subconscious mind with the association of pleasure to the habit, this positive association must be changed to a negative focused association, in order to stop the bad habit. We are often asked, "Who are you?" The simple answer is to tell the questioner your name. However, that does not really tell them who you are. The real answer is, "I am what I focus my subconscious mind on."

Three: Repeated negative or positive focused thoughts result in long-term organic change over time - When ill, negative, repeated, focused thoughts you have about yourself delay the healing process, and can even kill you with stress due to causing heart failure. When positive with uplifting thoughts, we tend to recover faster from illness. This is the mind and body connection being the same thing. A large percentage of human illnesses are functional as opposed to organic, so continued, negative, focused thoughts that you have about yourself, result in long-term, organic, negative change and therefore illness. The term used is "Psychosomatic" (illness caused by the mind).So, mind rule one and two develops into mind rule three, if the person continues the negative thoughts about them self. People that cause illness through the mind can be classed as neurotic, and the term used for a person that continuously has psychosomatic illness is a hypochondriac. Even though some people have genuine diseases, negative, repeated, focused thoughts will still result in further negative long-term organic change over time. With the use of hypnosis, the effect from the negative, focused thought can be changed, by changing the thought to positive. Be that as it may, a negative thought can also result in positive, organic change. For example: a negative thought towards the bad habit of smoking, means the organic change is better for long-term health due to the client avoiding smoking. Of course positive focused thoughts result in long-term positive health benefits for the mind and body.

Four: Imagination overpowers knowledge within in the mind - A smoker has the conscious knowledge that smoking is killing them, but yet they have not imagined the negative effects within the subconscious mind. The subconscious mind is therefore still playing a positive, imagined, associated movie toward the bad habit, and therefore the person does not change, because imagination has overpowered their knowledge, even though the positive association to the habit is wrong and is killing them. Once again remember that imagination (subconscious mind), is more powerful than knowledge (conscious mind), and the subconscious always wins, even when wrong. In order to do anything in life, you have to first imagine doing it, hence why imagination (subconscious mind), is more powerful than knowledge (conscious mind), within the whole mind. This is why people fail, they have made a conscious decision for change, and then tried to consciously succeed, but it is impossible to consciously stop smoking, lose weight, or any bad habit, when the subconscious is still playing a positive movie towards the bad habit. Change the positive to a negative within the subconscious and the bad habit is avoided. With regards to people with depression, anxiety, stress, low confidence etc, the movie within their subconscious is of wrongly believing an imagined, negative thought as fact. Example: a person may imagine that it is fact that they are useless, ugly etc, so they feel depressed and fear, even though they are wrong, but the negative, imagined thought is fact in their warped perception of reality. Change the imagined thought to agree with logic knowledge, and the person's reality changes for the positive and the problem is solved.

Five: Fixed thoughts can only be replaced by another via the subconscious - If every morning at 7am I got up and consciously made the decision to tap my head three times with my hand, the subconscious, eventually through repetition, takes the task on as a habit, it has become a fixed thought and it is incorporated into my morning ritual. This habit would then be protected by the subconscious. So to get up one morning and consciously force myself not to tap my head, would result in an overwhelming urge of anxiety, as if something is wrong, as if there is a potential danger. This anxiety of feeling there is a danger, is simply the subconscious mind reminding me to do the habit, because it wrongly feels it is doing me a favour protecting that habit, by keeping me from harm.

In order to overcome this anxiety, and to stop a potential danger, be it real or not, the subconscious reminds me of the habit, so I tap my head for instant relief from anxiety. In other words there is a subconscious resistance to change because the subconscious mind believes it is doing me a favour, so continues to protect the habit even though it is not healthy to do so. Remember the subconscious does not know the difference between a good or bad habit, it protects it regardless, as if there is a danger not to do so. It is simply an associated link between getting up in the morning and tapping my head that became a habit. In other words, repetition that has become a habit through an associated link. Changing the associated link subconsciously, will bring about permanent results.

For example, imagining myself getting up in the morning and doing press-ups, this would occupy my hands so as not to tap my head, and over time the press-ups become a new more positive habit. This is why a smoker always wants a cigarette first thing in the morning, due to the association of waking up and smoking, they have never imagined doing something else and not smoking.

Dear student, as far as the subconscious mind is concerned, what is the difference between the habit of smoking and the habit of me tapping my head? Think about that for a moment.

The answer is no difference, because both habits are protected within the subconscious, both create anxiety if not carried out, they are in fact the same. A habit. So now let me ask, what is the difference between smoking and swimming within the subconscious? The answer is they are the same, because both habits are protected, because the subconscious mind does not know the difference between swimming and smoking, both are a habit regardless of them being good or bad. The habit of swimming is protected to stop you from the danger of drowning if you fall in to a river, and the habit of smoking is protected to save you from potential danger that's not real. Your subconscious doesn't know there is no danger by not smoking, because the smoker has never told the subconscious mind of the danger of doing the habit in the first place. They have associated pleasure to it, so of course they keep smoking. The fixed thought that needs to be changed, needs to be replaced via the subconscious, because that is where the habit is stored, and not in the conscious mind, so of course consciously wanting to change will always result in failure, due to mind rule four: "Imagination overpowers knowledge within in the mind", and a combination of the other mind rules. You are starting to see how these seven mind rules are all connected, and of course they are, because we only have one mind each.

Six: Opposing ideas cannot be held at the same time - This means that once the subconscious has accepted an idea as fact, then any opposing conscious ideas will always be rejected. The subconscious, always conflicts against an opposing idea from the conscious mind, and as you know the subconscious is the stronger part of the mind and therefore, overpowers the opposing conscious idea or thought. That is true unless you change an idea on a subconscious level so that both parts of the mind are in agreement. For example: a person consciously thinks "I want to stop smoking", but they continue to smoke because their subconscious is protecting the habit and positive associated links of smoking, due to them not showing their subconscious any differently. Remember mind rule four: "Imagination overpowers knowledge within in the mind", which means the subconscious overpowers the conscious, and that of course has a detrimental effect on a person's life, and that is why, in order to change, it has to be done subconsciously first, to then be a conscious act. Also the subconscious cannot have two opposing ideas at the same time, for example: it cannot think fact (real) and fiction (not real), towards an idea at the same time, it is one or the other idea. The same with the conscious mind, you cannot logically think something is true and false at the same time. Nonetheless as you now know, the conscious can try to oppose an idea from the subconscious, but again, two opposing ideas cannot be held at the same time, so the stronger more powerful subconscious wins.

Seven: Conscious effort alone, results in opposite subconscious success - Conscious effort alone, results in opposite, subconscious success, means that; if you only consciously attempt to try and achieve your goal, you will fail every time. For example: a phobia client consciously thinks, "I don't want fear spiders" They have, by doing so, implanted within the subconscious mind, an image of them fearing a spider, the exact opposite of the conscious thought. So the client then feels fear due to the powerful suggestion of the image in their subconscious mind of doing so. If you say to yourself consciously "Don't think of a black cat", then subconsciously you have thought of one, the opposite of what you wanted to achieve. This is why conscious effort alone will never work to overcome a problem, and as you now know, the subconscious is more powerful than the conscious, and it overpowers the conscious will every time. This is why hypnosis is so successful in helping people overcome any problem.

Successfully Overcoming Fear and Phobia Session Explained

SUCCESSFULLY OVERCOMING PHOBIAS, and fear sessions are broken down into three parts:

1) Pre-talk
2) Suggestibility test
3) Hypnosis session

What is a Phobia?

Dear student, in order to fully understand the phobia script, I first need to explain to you what a phobia is. I will also share with you many examples of my real phobia clients that I have successfully treated in therapy.

Phobias are common of anxiety disorders. They are exaggerated fears due to going beyond what is seen as a: "Reasonable Concern" or "Normal Sense of Precaution." This is classed as neurosis. Phobias can develop in two different ways. Either from a startled response, or learned conditioned response, and I will explain these throughout this phobia book. I have mentioned startled response before with the example of the elderly man, who when he was a child fell in to the well (dark hole), who then saw a doctor once rescued. If you need to, then please go back and read the sub-chapter: "Free Association" in my Volume One Book.

To help you fully understand what a phobia is and how each of the two different ways develop (Startled or Conditioned), and how they affect a person, let us first look at this startled scenario. A child aged five is happily sleeping alone in a dark bedroom, when suddenly he is startled by a violent thunderstorm outside. This creates fear, because the child was asleep. Then, due to the loud thunder, the child was violently, startled and awoken. Even though previous to the storm, the child had happily been alone in the dark, the fear brought on by the loud thunder, can wrongly be associated to darkness within the subconscious mind, because the dark was the first thing the child saw on opening his eyes, and feeling fear at the same time from a startled response. The child's mind at the moment of the startled response, created an anchor and associated fear to it. There are one of two types of anchors that could have been created within the mind of the child. It can be either of the two types, but not both from the same event-cause. As I will now explain.

Anchor Type One causes the child from that night onwards to fears the dark, due to the created associated fear to darkness (anchor) that was brought on by a startled response from the thunder at the event-cause. So this: "Anchor Type One" response to the fear of darkness, means that from the night of the event-cause onwards, the continuation of darkness each night is just one specific need (darkness) for the reactivated "Anchor Type One," that triggers the associated fear emotion, which is classed as a phobia of the dark.

You may think that this child's reaction would also cause him to fear thunder, or even loud noises separately from the dark anchor. However an associated fear cannot be associated to two different anchors at the same time from the same event-cause. The emotional fear caused from the startled response (thunder bang) was associated to the dark, due to the child first seeing the dark on awakening, and by then the loud bang had stopped. If another loud bang occurs then the child would either compound the fear on to the dark anchor, or the emotion would be associated to a loud bang anchor from darkness, which is a reassociation of emotion.

Anchor Type One in a person's mind, can allow them to remember the memory from the event that caused (event-cause) the trauma, or it can repress the memory. Regardless of whether the memory is remembered or repressed, the fear emotion associated to the anchor (darkness) remains triggered each night with an: "Anchor Type One" reaction. Of course, if the one specific need to reactivate an: "Anchor Type One" was something that didn't happen regularly, then of course the associated fear emotion would remain dormant until the anchor was reactivated, and that could be months later. But let's stick to my example of the child in the dark, as I explain the: "Anchor Type Two."

"Anchor Type Two" causes the child's subconscious mind, from the moment of the event-cause onwards, to repress the memory of the event-cause, and for many years into adulthood, this repressed memory of the event-cause, due to the traumatic nature attached to it, remains hidden. Of course this can also happen with "Anchor Type One" as well in some cases, as I will later explain. However the difference with "Anchor Type Two" is that the anchor with the associated emotional fear remains, but is not reactivated for many years, so throughout childhood to early adulthood, he has continued to be very happy in the dark alone. Unlike: "Anchor Type One" where he felt fear every night to the dark.

Dear student, why is the anchor with the associated emotional fear not reactivated for years with an: "Anchor Type Two" considering he has, since the event-cause, been alone in the dark whilst "Anchor Type One" was reactivated every night after the event-cause, even though the memory can still remain repressed? An interesting question, so please give it some thought before reading on.

Simple. Because the anchor that triggers the fear with an: "Anchor Type Two" is associated to two different simultaneous specific needs (dark and noise), and so both need to occur at the same time, which has since not happened. The first specific need: it has to be dark. And the second: at the same time there has to be a loud bang. The two occurring different simultaneous specific needs (dark and noise) together, are the one anchor to the associated fear from the event-cause. If both specific needs (dark and noise) occur at the same time, at any point from the date of the event-cause, then the: "Anchor Type Two" is reactivated and therefore the associated emotion of fear is triggered.

Of course many years could pass before that happens, so hence why the person has no phobia for many years when being in the dark, due to no loud noise happening at the same time. So, in my example of the child in the dark, "Anchor Type Two" requires two different simultaneous specific needs (dark and noise) and therefore, the emotions of fear are delayed for years, as the anchor remains none active until both specific needs are confronted at the same time. "Anchor type one" required only one specific need (darkness) to reactivate the anchor, but it is more likely for: "Anchor Type One" to happen sooner in my example, due to only one specific need being required, which happens every night. "Anchor Type Two" is delayed for years, due to two simultaneous specific needs being required, that for this person, has not happened yet.

Dear student, to recap. The: "Anchor Type One" after the event-cause, needed the one specific need occurring, which was that of darkness as the anchor, hence why associated fear was felt every night after the event-cause. "Anchor Type Two" needs two simultaneous specific needs (dark and noise) occurring at the same time, that is one anchor to trigger the associated emotion of fear (the phobia) from the one event-cause. Hence the long delay into adulthood before the fear is triggered, because the anchor had previously not been reactivated. This is because the two simultaneous specific needs (dark and noise) had not occurred together until adulthood.

Now look at the response of anchor type one and two again. They both, in fact, have the same reaction to the associated emotional fear, and the event-cause memory being repressed is a totally separate issue from either anchor type. Yet, if the memory had not been repressed, but seemingly forgotten, or not thought about for a while, then once an anchor is reactivated, a person can remember the memory and the emotion attached at the same time. Both anchor types can have a delayed reactivation. Even so: "Anchor Type One" is more likely to be reactivated sooner than: "Anchor Type Two" due to only one specific need required.

Some psychotherapists will argue that the dark and the loud bang, are two different anchors associated to the same fear from the same event-cause. Nonetheless that is total nonsense, because if that was the case, then humans would never encounter the: "Anchor Type Two" from an event-cause, because all phobic's would then only have an: "Anchor Type One" and that is not the case at all. Think about it. The child was never scared of loud noises, so that could not have been a separate: "Anchor Type One." This proves that: "Anchor Type Two" is one anchor and not two different anchors. The one anchor requires two different simultaneous specific needs (dark and noise) occurring at the same time, to trigger the association of fear from the event-cause, and is not two different anchors. There is no such thing as two anchors being reactivated to provoke an associated emotion from the same event-cause. Imagine if there was. This person would constantly fear the same emotion from the same event-cause and associate it to noise (first anchor) and the dark (second anchor) separately, so there would be no: "Anchor Type Two" within a person's mind, and I know: "Anchor Type Two" is a response that people have of needing two simultaneous specific needs for one anchor. Of course people can fear the dark and noises separately, but not with each having the same associated emotion attached from the same event-cause. It would be impossible to function in life if we as humans associated the same fear to different anchors from the same event-cause, because that would be a nightmare, and never happens because the mind simply doesn't allow it to happen. From one event-cause there is only one anchor associated to an emotion from that event-cause, and not two different anchors reactivating to trigger the same emotion. Still as you now know there are two types of anchors, and no, there is not a third type of anchor!

Be that as it may, remember that there can still be two different associations to one anchor, those being memory and the emotion from the same event-cause. Either both are remembered, or just the emotion, once the anchor is reactivated. Also remember that a reactivated anchor that triggers a memory never does so without the emotion as well. But an emotion can be triggered without the memory, due to the memory being repressed. Any memories that you have that you remember, but you cannot remember the emotion from the same event as well, then that memory was not triggered by a reactivated anchor. It was just a memory that you remembered in the form of a habit, due to thinking of the same memory regularly. Think about that, because that has got your brain cells working on over drive hasn't it? It needs more thought in order to sink in to your subconscious.

Dear student, have you ever read that in any other book on this subject? I know you haven't, so it is your choice on whether you agree with me or not. The same can be said for most things I am teaching you in this book. The subject matter maybe the same in other books, but my take on psychotherapy and human psychology is unique in many aspects. So the choice is yours on whether you like and agree with what I am teaching you.

Keeping with the child scenario in the dark example, if the child did not see darkness ever again after the event-cause and the memory had been repressed of the event-cause, then of course there would never be a phobic emotional response of: "Anchor Type One" or "Two" because they would never be reactivated, and because the person does not consciously know they fear the dark, due to the repressed memory, and the anchor was never subconsciously reactivated. They live a life of no reaction of feeling the fear that was created, but remained dormant from the time of the event-cause onwards. With regards to my example, that cannot happen, because a person cannot avoid the dark, so even if the person doesn't consciously know they fear the dark, their subconscious will still remind them when in the dark, due to the reactivated: "Anchor Type One."

Anyhow, if the: "Anchor Type One" was that of seeing a snake that was created from a startled response when on holiday in a country with wild snakes. Then of course, if the memory was repressed and the: "Anchor Type One" was never reactivated again, so it remained dormant, because the person went home to a country with no wild snakes, then there would never be a phobic response as if the event-cause never happened. Unless of course the person went to a zoo and saw a snake because then: "Anchor Type One" would be reactivated. Obviously a snake can be avoided in most countries, unlike darkness, but if the person doesn't know to avoid snakes, because they don't consciously know they fear them, due to the repressed memory from an event-cause of a startled response of seeing a snake, then the: "Anchor Type One" remains dormant. But the subconscious takes over in reminding them of the associated fear due to the reactivated: "Anchor Type One" of seeing a snake in a zoo, which could be years after the event-cause.

So if the person, years later after the event-cause, saw a snake in the zoo, they change from having no conscious recollection of fear of snakes, to feeling the feared emotion from the event-cause, due to the reactivated: "Anchor Type One" which only needed one specific need to be reactivated, which is that of seeing a snake, this triggered the fear emotion from the event-cause. But remember that the memory is still being repressed, so they will have no idea why they have had the fear reaction to seeing a snake, or the memory is now remembered, if the person is ready to come to terms with the past memory, but that is unlikely without therapy. I will in a moment give a real example of a person that had a fear of heights, but did not consciously know, due to the repressed memory of the event-cause and the dormant associated fear due to the anchor not being reactivated for years.

For now let's continue with the snake fear. A person with a fear of snakes could have an: "Anchor Type Two" with the two simultaneous specific needs being required. One specific need is that the snake has to be seen, and two, the snake has to be touched, meaning that one of the specific needs without the other would not cause a phobic response on its own. I had a client with a fear of spiders and the two simultaneous specific needs were required as an: "Anchor Type Two" to trigger the fear. One the spider had to be large, and two, it had to be seen moving to reactivate the: "Anchor Type Two" to the associated fear. When she looked at a small spider it did not bother her at all, so she did not have an: "Anchor Type One" from the event-cause, because two simultaneous specific needs were needed in order to feel the emotional fear. Of course there is another reaction from an event-cause that can happen, and that is the person doesn't need to have created an: "Anchor Type One" or

"Two", the person is not bothered because they are able to calm down after a startled response, so no associated fear to an anchor is ever created. This type of reaction is a person that is an: option three person, which is a person that has already (cognitively) subconsciously rehearsed, and physically rehearsed where possible, with every traumatic situation they can think of as described in chapter: "Abreactions" in my Volume One Book, and earlier in this chapter too.

Using the same example of the child in the dark. Once this child grows up to be an adult, let's say aged thirty five and then this new scenario happens. He is in his lounge one night and his wife is preparing a meal in the kitchen (no I'm not sexist, the person in the kitchen could be his gay lover for all I care). Suddenly there is a power cut and all the lights go dark. The sudden shock of the darkness causes his wife to drop a pan, which makes a loud noise as it hits the floor. This may reactivate that past: "Anchor Type Two" with the associated emotion of feeling fear in the man's mind. This is due to the two simultaneous specific needs (dark and noise) happening at the same time, which is the anchor to trigger the associated fear. This thirty five years young adult, is now responding to the fear through the mind of a child aged five, because that is the age of the associated fear to the anchor. Regardless, he still does not know why he feels the fear, because the memory from childhood is still repressed. So it is only the triggered emotional fear of a child aged five from the reactivated: "Anchor Type Two" that is remembered, and not the memory of the event from childhood which caused the fear in the first place. Unless of course, he is ready to come to terms with the memory, but without therapy that would be hard, so the memory remains repressed. The man's lack of understanding of the fear he is feeling creates more fear because he cannot understand why he is acting like a child, even though he is an adult. He doesn't know that the subconscious has no concept of time, and so without skilful therapy help, the fear will remain and get worse. This man will also have no conscious thought as to what triggered the fear, because he won't understand that two simultaneous specific needs (dark and noise) occurred, that affected his subconscious anchor to trigger the fear, and again that lack of understanding creates even more fear. From that day forward he will have a phobia of whatever he reassociates the fear to, because that fear now has to be associated to something else in order for the victim to try and understand. This is a reassociation of the emotion and that could be to anything, maybe to just darkness: "Anchor Type One" due to the power cut, or even his dog jumping up at him. Previously he had no fear of dogs, but now he does, due to the reassociated emotion of fear to the new different anchor of a dog. All this overwhelms the person and is very confusing for the mind of a man that lacks understanding of his own mind, and who has no psychotherapy knowledge of the mind model as you now have. I have given examples of reassociated emotions within this book, but with this example the: "Anchor Type Two" that triggered the fear, was replaced with the: "Anchor Type One" to the same fear, but with a different specific need to reactivate the new anchor.

Dear student, this is a very important note that you must remember. Over the years, through working with many phobics, I have discovered that the memory of the event that caused the phobia is repressed, because ninety percent of phobic's have no idea why they fear what they have a phobic response to. So it is only the emotion generated by the associated fear once the anchor is reactivated, that is reawakened and not the memory of the origins of the phobia from the event-cause. This does not mean the person is consciously aware of the associated anchor, because they may not be, but their subconscious mind is, and the fear, once triggered, is real to them, even though it is irrational. Of course I find the origins of the phobia from using my version of: "Free Association" in a session with a client, however this chapter of the book is explaining what a phobia is and how they develop and not how I find it. I have already in detail explained in the sub-chapter: "Free Association" in the Volume One Book of how I find the repressed memory event-cause and I have briefly explained the cure.

So why are memories repressed, and the emotional fear associated to the anchor reawakened (emotion remembered) once the anchor is reactivated? I write: "Emotional fear associated to the anchor reawakened" because again, that doesn't mean the anchor is consciously remembered or known to the person once reactivated, even though the emotion is felt. Remember that all our emotions are stored within our subconscious and not conscious, and anchors that trigger emotions or memories (or both), are stored subconsciously as well, so they are not always consciously known, and that is why some clients don't fully understand what triggered the fear, because it happens on a subconscious level and not a conscious one. Some clients will even create a false memory of the cause to try and understand their emotions, in an attempt to relieve their fear, but that just creates more confusion and long-term more fear as a result. An example of this will be shared with you later. Back to the question of: Why are memories repressed and the emotional fear associated to the anchor reawakened (emotion remembered) once the anchor is reactivated? I have already mentioned why memories are repressed, and why the fear associated to the anchor is reawakened once the anchor is reactivated. Even so, allow me to explain another way. Remember in the chapter: "Abreactions", from my Volume One Book, the electric kettle analogy? The mind being an electric kettle. Once the temperature gets too hot it shuts off as the thermostat protects the kettle from overheating, hence the term kettle effect. If a person's mind experiences an event of a traumatic nature, then it may be too: "Hot" for that person's mind to handle. So their subconscious represses that memory and locks it deep within the subconscious mind or the fourth part of the mind in which I previously named the: "Repressed Suppressed Area." However, the fearful emotion associated to the anchor is lying dormant and waiting to be triggered once the right anchor is reactivated, from the specific needs of seeing a spider for example, this is because the subconscious wants to protect the person from any possible future danger be it real or imagined danger. So, with my example, when confronted by thunder or a loud noise and darkness again the associated anchor reawakens, but not the memory of the event, until it is found in a session. The mind of the adult reverts back to the same emotions that he had as a child, from the frightening time in the bedroom, all alone, feeling the fear once again from an associated anchor and not the memory of the origins (event-cause) of the phobia. As an adult, the phobic feels ashamed of feeling like a child all helpless and confused. The phobia is rationalised through the mind of a child, because that is where the mind reverts back to, because the emotional associated trigger is still that of a child from when it was formed. Remember that an associated emotion to an anchor does not age. The person's physical body has aged but not the emotion, because that is a state of mind. This is why it is very difficult for an adult to admit to a phobia and get help, because they are embarrassed of acting like a child. It is a very frightening experience as an adult to suddenly feel all the emotions of a child's mentality overwhelm you and not understand why.

Dear student, I know I was repeating myself in different ways in my explanation of phobias, and the reason being is because that is the best way to feed your subconscious the information, so that you will remember. And it is the best way when talking to clients; repeat, repeat and repeat again if you need to, as you explain to your clients. Also repeating the same information in slightly different ways eliminates any misunderstanding of the information and so is a great way of teaching, and if you like the way I teach them you must agree.

Remember the four options that can happen within a person's mind in and after a traumatic situation? Read them again and think which option fits: "Anchor Type One" from my example of the boy in the dark, and which option fits: "Anchor Type Two":

Fright response consumes the persons mind, and they could potentially die as the event is taking place, or if they survive they can no longer function in life. The only way to survive a fright response is by being dragged out of the situation by another person and later being helped through therapy. This type of person cannot help them self and they could be very vulnerable to suggestion, depending on their level of fright. The deeper the level, the less suggestible they are, because they won't react at all, as if frozen with fear.

The situation is so traumatic that the person's mind represses the memory from the event-cause, and after the event they go about their day as if nothing has happened. They survive the initial event, but later the emotion that is associated to the anchor, can at any given time, be reactivated and so they abreact. Also the traumatic memory, can after an event, be remembered as well, but that is rare without controlled therapy. This person then becomes the first option, if professional help is not given to them.

The person has already (cognitively), subconsciously rehearsed, and physically rehearsed where possible with every traumatic situation they can think of. That way the chance of survival with having a strong proactive mind is greatly increased. This does not mean that an abreaction won't occur at some point in the future, long after the event. This is because at the event, the person is in subconscious auto pilot and not consciously aware, then days, months or years later, they may become consciously aware that the event took place, which may cause an abreaction even, though that is unlikely. Or they may simply, after the event, be consciously aware and except it and move on with their life. This option covers: "Fight or Flight Responses", of how a person prevents the response.

With this forth option the person does not know they are in danger, so they don't realise that it should be a traumatic event to them, and therefore the forth option reaction in a person's mind is that they just carry on as if nothing has happened. Again this type of person's reaction makes them vulnerable to suggestion. A good example of option four is a child getting into a stranger's car, and this option four person can change into option one or two, due to them later realising the danger as their situation gets worse.

"Anchor Type One" from my example of the boy in the dark clearly triggers: "Option One" of what can happen within a person's mind in what they wrongly see as a traumatic situation. The only difference is that the fright response is only triggered when in the dark and so the boy functions normally in all other situations. Alternatively: "Option Two" of what can happen within a person's mind in and after what they see as a traumatic situation, can happen with: "Anchor Type One." Now think what options could happen with: "Anchor Type Two," and give that some thought before reading on. Obviously the emotion is the same regardless of the anchor type, because the event-cause is the same and therefore the same options that: "Anchor Type One" triggers are also triggered with: "Anchor Type Two."

Dear student by now you will have realised why I have structured this book the way that I have. Each chapter links to other chapters and sub-chapters throughout this book. It is a way of keeping you interested and engaged, wanting to read on and learn more, without bombarding your mind all at once on one topic, which would have been too overwhelming and confusing. I feel it is the best way for me to teach you, and therefore the best way for you to learn. This way the whole book must be read before you can fully appreciate and understand the knowledge that I am passing on to you, as I continue to drip feed my knowledge from my own experiences of life and from working with my clients.

Many years ago I climbed to the top of the ancient Chichen Itza Pyramid in Mexico. I was privileged because the general public are no longer allowed that same experience. Once on the top, I ran around taking pictures of the view and was very confident, because I knew that if I fell then the furthest I would drop was down to the next step. Each step was less than a meter in height and the same in width, so little harm would have come to me if I had fallen down the climbable steps. Be that as it may, at the corners of the pyramid the steps are seventeen meters in height, so of course I was more careful at the corners. It therefore seems odd that no one else rationalised that, because the people at the top with me started to scream in horror. They wrongly assumed that because we were thirty meters high off the ground, they thought that if I fell I would fall the full thirty meters to the ground and die. That of course was not a logical thought process, due to the size of the steps, and a pyramid is not a sheer vertical cliff face drop of thirty meters. Yes we were high but logically in my mind only as high as the next step. If you looked directly down from the top all you could see were huge steps going down to the ground at an obvious angle, so it was safe enough to run around.

One man I watched, confidently climbed to the top whilst he was looking forwards at the steps. But once at the top, he turned around and looked out at the distant view, and at that moment he realised he was high up from the ground so his subconscious mind reawakened an: "Anchor Type One" with the association of fear of heights. This reactivated anchor caused him to have the emotions of a child, and he crumbled to his knees screaming and crying as if he was an infant. He was completely inconsolable, like a child possessed with overwhelming fear. The reactivated anchor only required one specific need being present to reactivate the anchor and that need was height. He was that of: "Option One" with what happens within a person's mind in a traumatic situation, which is fright. In this case the situation he is now in with the associated fear from a reactivated anchor that was created from a previous event-cause situation from when he was a child. He was initially: "Option Two" with the memory from a previous event-cause being repressed and the anchor being dormant. However once the anchor was reactivated within his subconscious, it caused him to have the mindset of: "Option One" even though the event-cause memory is still repressed.

Dear student, how do I know that the fear he is feeling on top of the pyramid is not the event-cause of his fear, it is just a reaction from a previous event-cause, in the form of a reactivated anchor with the association of fear to heights? I know for a fact that his fear is from are activated anchor that was created from a previous event-cause in his past of fear from heights, and not from the present startled response of him realising he is high at the top of a pyramid as the event-cause of fear. So my question put another way is: How do I know his fear is from an anchor that has been reactivated in the situation he is in, and not from his present situation of being on top of the pyramid as the event-cause of fear? Give it some thought before reading on.

The answer is simple. It is clear to me that his emotional reaction of fear was that of a child and not an adult even, though he is an adult in the present tense. The explanation for that is because as a child he must have been startled by a great height, so the associated emotional fear to the anchor of heights was that of a child that was reactivated, which had consumed his adult's mind on the pyramid with the mentality of a child. Remember that associated links do not age, because they are a state of mind and not the physical body, and also the subconscious has no concept of time with regards to associated links. That explains why he has the emotions of a child in his present situation from a previous event-cause, because he had been a child at the event-cause of fear which is now affecting his adult mind. Also the memory of the childhood traumatic event-cause which created the fear of heights must have been repressed within his mind. I know this because if the memory had not been repressed, then he would not have climbed up the pyramid, because he would have consciously remembered that he feared heights. So for years the person did not consciously know he feared heights, until the anchor was reactivated from being high, but by then it is too late to avoid the situation of being at the top of a high pyramid. So once again as a result of the repressed memory, he clearly did not know he feared heights until at the top of the pyramid when the anchor was reactivated with the associated emotion of overwhelming childlike fear attached. Not only was a childhood anchor reactivated, and of course I know this due to him acting like a child, but also in the man's mind he had confused distant from the view to height. In the fright state that he was in, his logical conscious mind had ceased to function, so he could not rationalise the situation as an adult and therefore could not calm down. With him being in an option one mindset of fright, without help, that man would have remained frozen with fear and would have died. He had to therefore be helped down by being surrounded by people, so that he could not see the view or the ground, but even so, he screamed all the way down.

Dear student, you know why a traumatic memory is repressed and why the associated emotion to the anchor remains waiting to be triggered at any given time in the future. Still I have another question for you – Years after an event, when the reactivated anchor triggers or reawakens the associated emotion attached to the anchor, why is the repressed memory not also remembered at the same time as feeling the associated emotion? It seems logical to think that even though the memory was repressed at the time of the traumatic event, and considering the emotional associated anchor was created at the same moment of the traumatic event happening, then both the emotion and the memory should now be known to the person when the reactivated anchor is present. So why doesn't the anchor once reactivated also allow a person to remember the previously repressed memory as well as the emotion? Interesting question, so please give it some thought before reading on.

The simple answer is because the anchor only has an association to an emotion from the traumatic event and not the memory of the event that created the emotion, because the memory is still repressed and therefore is separate from the associated emotional anchor. So hence why the memory is not remembered once the anchor is reactivated. Only the emotion of fear reawakens to warn the person of potential danger. A memory and an emotion are two separate things, even though both are created form the same event. If the memory is repressed then that is why people can take one emotion that was created from an event and associate that same emotion to a different event, be it a real or an imagined event. In other words an emotion can be associated to a different memory or false memories (false-truth) if the event-cause memory is repressed. Or the emotion can even be associated to a different anchor without the person being consciously aware of it, and that can cause problems, but it can happen due to a coping mechanism of the person not wanting to except or take responsibility for the real cause of the emotion due to the upsetting nature of it. Or even as previously explained, the lack of understand of the emotion and not knowing what the anchor is. The person has to associate the emotion to something and further examples with be shown within this book. I have previously mentioned this, of course if a memory was not repressed but seemingly forgotten, or not thought about for a while, then once an anchor is reactivated, a person can remember the memory and the emotion attached at the same time, because an anchor can have two associations with those being memory and emotion, but not two emotions or two memories.

Another scenario is of a youngster that is startled when mauled by a dog, and so from that day forwards a phobia of dogs is present in the victim's subconscious mind due to the associated feared anchor reactivating every time they see a dog. Phobias can also be conditioned (learned) into a child from the parents or other adults. The learned phobia tends to start in childhood, where the child's parents are, for example: afraid of dogs and so the child learns to fear dogs. This develops into a phobia, due to the conditioning that becomes a habit to feel fear associations towards dogs. Both causes of phobias, either conditioned (learned) or startled responses, are treated in the same way as I will explain later. The client needs to know whether the phobia originated from a startled or conditioned response, so that they understand the event-cause, because understanding relieves tension, and it is important that you find the cause so that you can treat the effect. Once the cause is known the client will have a sense of release from the phobia. It is unheard of that an adult of sound mind having a phobia conditioned into them, so most adults form a recent phobia from a startled response. However if an adult is suggestible, due to being vulnerable with depression for example, then and only then can an adult be conditioned to have a phobia. So if a phobia is recent within an adult, then the cause could be a reactivated anchor from childhood that had previously remained dormant for years until the specific need is present to reawaken the anchor, or the phobia can be a startled response. If the adult has a resent phobia that is neither of those two causes, then you know they are highly suggestible, due to a conditioned fear and therefore they could have hidden issues of stress etc. Of course a person with stress can even condition a phobia into their own subconscious mind, with the emotional fear from stress being reassociated to something else, because they don't want to come to term with what is stressing them out, and therefore a phobia is created of the something else, whatever it maybe.

I was walking with two mates in town one night when one jokingly put the other in a head lock under his arm. This instantly reactivated a feared associated anchor within my mate's mind that was in the head lock and he reverted back to being a child. He started to cry and begged my other mate to stop, even though he was just messing about and not physically hurting him. It later emerged that my mate, who was crying, was several years ago, put in to a head lock as a child by a stranger who mugged him of his birthday money when he was out shopping. His subconscious mind, now as an adult, had realised that he was in a similar situation walking past shops then being in a head lock, this reactivated the anchor with the associated emotion to fear from the past, because his mind thinks it is doing him a favour as a protection mechanism. His subconscious is simply reminding him how he felt the last time he was in that situation, and therefore was warning him of a potential danger, even though one was not present to him. If not dealt with, this could develop further into a phobia of watching other people put their arms around one another, and that is how simple it is for a phobia to be created. Within all phobia sessions always associate good feeling to an anchor as will be explained later. Then with the good feeling anchor walk them through a situation where in the past they would have had a phobic response, more will be explained as we continue.

Examples of Real Phobia Clients

Dear student, now that you understand more about phobias, before I explain the pre-talk, I will give you some examples of phobia clients that I have treated successfully, which will help you understand even more, and by the end of this book you will know everything that there is to know on this whole subject.

I received a phone call from a woman aged thirty two who was terrified when touched in her sleep. Once touched, she would suddenly awaken feeling fear, but she had no idea why. At first you would think that this could be a sexual problem, or maybe she had been sexually abused when she was a child, but that was not the case as I found out in the pre-talk by asking the right questions.

In fact, now as an adult, she had a good sex life. Even so she would still feel fear, even if her boyfriend put his arm around her in a nonsexual way once she was asleep or trying to sleep. Having read this book to this point, you will know that most people suffering from phobias have no memory of why or how the phobia started in the first place (the event-cause), but in most cases the phobia originates from childhood. You also know that it is best to use my version of free association in the pre-talk with this client to reawaken the repressed memory. I do this because once the client remembers the source of the problem; they can then deal with it due to understanding it. When free associating with this client, I first needed to eliminate the boyfriend from the investigation to the cause, or find out if he was the cause. So I asked how long she had the problem, and the answer given to me gave me a time frame back to childhood, before the client had met her boyfriend. As a result I eliminated him from the event-cause and I now knew that this phobia originated as a child.

My thought on this phobia was that it was probably created from a startled response to being woken from sleep by being touched as a child when she wasn't expecting to be touched. That leads me to think that she slept alone in her bedroom so hence why she wasn't expecting anyone to touch her. In order to know whether my thoughts were correct or not I asked did anyone else she knew or knows of have the same phobia and the answer was no, so that reply validated my thought of the cause as being startled and not conditioned. I also asked did she sleep alone in her bedroom and again the answer was in agreement to my thoughts, that of yes. However that does not eliminate other places she could have slept as a child that could have been the source of the event-cause of the phobia, so I make a note in my mind of the next questions to ask in relation to my new thought. I also knew without the client telling me, that the original touch that caused the phobia, could not have been a gentle touch to slowly awaken her; it must have been violent to have caused a startled response phobia. This got me thinking, where does a child tend to sleep? The options are at home, or Grandparents or at a friend's house or even on holiday somewhere, so I needed to eliminate the places where the phobia was not created. I asked the client can she remember the first time she felt fear and the answer was at home, of course that doesn't mean the client is right, but it does give me a possible starting point. I asked her who she lived with as a child and it emerged that she was an only child living with her mum. This eliminates the cause from any brothers, sisters or dad and makes my job easier. Continuing my investigation with using my version of free association, I discovered that her mother was an alcoholic. It emerged that as a young child my client would be left alone in the house at night when her alcoholic mother was at the local bar. As a child my client would fall asleep and once her drunken mother returned home in the early hours of the morning she would enter the child's bedroom and wake her by violently shaking her. Her mother would awaken her and force her to do all the housework with no thought to the damage she was doing to her daughter by startling her in that way. Just imagine being that child asleep then having someone grab and shake you in the dark. Is it any wonder that a phobia was created by a startled response and then conditioned into my client by repetition from the mother's behaviour? Previous to the session with me it is also understandable why my client's subconscious had repressed the traumatic memory that I was able to reawaken.

A very successful outcome was achieved with this client, and the pre-talk alone was enough in light trance to cure the client's phobia. The phobia was removed once my client had an explanation to the event-cause of her fear. She was so relieved by simply understanding the source of her problem, that now, as an adult, she realised that the fear was now an irrational one, because her mother could no longer abuse her in that way. The reason being was because the threat had been taken away, due to the client no longer living with her mother and the fear from lack of understanding was gone. As a result, the client's mind was now at rest and there was no need to use deep hypnosis.

Dear student, this has been a really good example of a client's reawakened memory that was previously repressed, and the benefits of allowing the client's mind to be aware of the memory, even though a slight but temporary abreaction occurs once the memory is known.

An adult female client I treated in therapy came because she cried every time she saw someone eat. Just the thought of watching someone's mouth chew food would make her cry. She had started a new office job and the woman on the next desk to her would eat her dinner at the desk, which would cause my client to cry. This was obviously affecting her life and work to the point where she was thinking of leaving her new job. The same as many phobic clients, she had no idea why she was having this phobic response to a simple, everyday activity of people eating and she had this phobia from childhood. From experience, I knew this phobia was not conditioned because it was so unusual, so it had to be caused from a startled response from childhood. Of course once again, the same as my last example, I asked the question did she know of anyone else with the same phobia, as I needed to validate my thoughts and I was proven right. It was also obvious to me that as a child she already felt fear from a startled response before she had seen people eating, so her subconscious had wrongly reassociated the emotional fear she already felt to watching people eating (anchor). I knew that because the phobia was not conditioned and it would have been highly unlikely to be startled by watching someone eat. There is nothing fearful about watching people eat, so that could not have been the event-cause, the cause was repressed, but the emotional fear from the cause was reassociated to seeing people eat (anchor) because the emotion had to go somewhere.

There are two main places where a child eats, one at home and the other at school, so using my version of free association I eliminated the place of the non-cause which was school. I did that by simply asking the client about the first memory she had of feeling the fear, and it was at home. Of course she could be wrong, but again it gave me a starting point to work with. Without the client knowing, I knew for a fact that something happened that she considered to be traumatic and then she sat down for a meal with other people eating around her. The odds are this was a family meal and because the phobia was of watching people eat, the traumatic event that caused the emotional fear must have happened minutes before a meal to be quickly reassociated to watching people eat. It must have happened quickly because if not, then she would have associated the fear to something else. This knowledge from experience eliminated all possible causes apart from one. I knew an accident could not have happened to cause the fear because the family wouldn't have sat down to eat straight after a traumatic accident. The cause could not have been anything more than a family argument just before a meal and then soon after they all sat down at the dining table to eat where no one was talking. Hence why her mind focused the fear onto watching people eat, which is a reassociated emotion of fear from a startled response from a family argument that she was not expecting to happen.

In that situation I also knew the television could not have been on or any music, because if there had been then she would have been watching the TV or listening to music and her mind would have associated the fear to whatever was on TV or what she was listening to, so I knew there had to have been total silence for her mind to focus on people eating, hence how I also know no one was talking. To validate my thoughts I asked her was there many family arguments as a child before a meal and the answer was, yes.

Previously at the early stages of the session I had explained the mind model to the client and what a phobia was, this made free association easier in finding the cause of the phobia due to her mind understanding what a phobia is and the two causes which are conditioned or startled. So she slowly put everything into place within her mind which was being helped by what I was saying and from the relaxed state she was in. So with the client having the knowledge given to her and my questions, she realised the event-cause of the phobia. Due to the client's relaxed state and new knowledge, what had been a previous repressed memory was now known to her, and also because she now realised the event-cause is no longer of any threat to her. I knew this because I could see the revelation hitting her like a wave of relief in her body language and facial expression. So without her telling me, I told her my thoughts and she was amazed, as if I was reading her mind from a forgotten memory. The events that led up to the origins of the phobia emerged.

There had been a huge family argument between brothers, sisters, mum and dad and this was the upsetting traumatic event for my client from when she had been a child. The family then all sat, down to eat but no one was talking due to the previous argument. At that point, as a child, my client's mind would have been confused and fearful and that emotion has to be associated to something, so she focused her attention on watching people eat, which became the anchor to trigger fear. Hence the fearful emotion associated to the anchor of watching people eat that affected her in adult life, in the form of a phobia.

Dear student I'm sure you agree by now that phobias and how people create them are fascinating, but simple to understand.

Another example. I treated a female adult client who had a phobic response to enclosed spaces. Her main problem was at work, because her work colleagues would get the buildings lift to the office's higher floor and she would walk up several flights of stairs in order to avoid a phobic response from being in an enclosed lift. As a result she was late for meetings and out of breath on arrival. This became more of a problem when she went to other office buildings for meetings, because the staff there didn't know about her phobia. This caused her embarrassment and again she would be the last in the meeting and out of breath due to walking up all the stairs and that made her look unprofessional due to being late, even so she was still very successful in business.

In the pre-talk with the use of my version of free association therapy, it emerged that the event-cause of the phobia was from playing: "Hide and Seek" as a child. As a child she had decided to hide in a cupboard, and her sister then realised where she was hidden and so she locked her in the enclosed space. As a result fear set in to my client's mind when she was a child due to not expecting to be trapped. So a startled response developed into a phobia later in life. In just one session the phobia had been removed and I did that by simply reassociating the emotion of pleasure from her past (timeline technique with anchoring) to being in a lift, which replaced the original fear association to the same anchor of being in an enclosed space. This is what I did. As a child this client found the Muppet Show to be funny and so she had associations of pleasure towards the theme tune and Kermit the Frog. Whilst the client was under hypnosis I built on this good feeling within her mind by pretending to be Kermit the Frog whilst talking to the client and whilst making the sound of the theme tune to the Muppet Show. That good emotional feeling of childlike fun flooded her subconscious and then I reassociated that emotion to the anchor of getting into a lift and remaining there as the lift doors closed etc. In her mind this of course was a real experience and she had achieved her goal whilst feeling really good about it. So because her subconscious thought she had now been in an enclosed space whilst feeling happy about it, it was easy for her after the session to go into an enclosed space in real life because her subconscious simply reminded her of the pleasurable emotions that were now associated to the anchor of being in a small space. Once again this is the mind model of the subconscious not knowing the difference between what is real or imagined. It was as simple as that to remove the original association of fear, and remember that the subconscious cannot have two opposing associations to the same thought, so the new pleasurable one had replaced the fear, and that, once again, goes back to the mind model information.

Three years after the session, I received a phone call from this client's sister, and the main thing she said to me was: "I have just been on holiday with my sister and I was amazed that she got into a lift with me and she started to jump up and down in the lift with the doors closed. She then told me about you and so I would like to book an appointment."

I booked this sister in for a confidence boost with regards to her work meetings, in order to help her achieve more within the company that she worked for. What is amazing about these two sisters is that first of all they were identical twins, and second, both had developed different problems from playing the same game: "Hide and Seek" together as children. The first had developed a phobia of enclosed spaces and the second sister had developed low confidence in achieving more in business. This was fascinating to me because both had a different problem developed from playing the same game together as children, but yet both were being affected in the work place with regards to business and meetings, even though effected differently in the work place, with the first sister being late and embarrassed in meetings and the other lacking confidence in meetings.

Let me break it down in simple terms to make it easier for me to explain, and for you to understand these two sisters, and their problems from the playing the same game, with both having a different event-cause outcome.

First sister - Playing Hide and Seek as a child develops a phobia of enclosed spaces due to being locked in a cupboard. Even though she was successful in business, the phobia affected her work by being late for meetings, feeling embarrassed and out of breath, due to avoiding the lift and having to walk up several flights of stairs.

Second sister - Playing Hide and Seek as a child develops guilt within her mind, due to being better than her sister at the game. She felt ashamed, guilty and regretted causing her sister to develop a bad phobia. This caused the second sister to take a step back in life as they grew up, in order to allow her sister to be better than her in other aspects of life. Clearly this second sister did this to alleviate her guilt that had built up from childhood, but over time this affected the second sister's confidence in business meetings and generally in the work place. That is the reason why she was not as successful as her sister in business.

The first sister had the phobia, but yet was more successful than the second sister in business, which is what the second sister had wanted for her twin in order to dilute her own guilt. The second sister even told me that not only had she locked her sister in a cupboard as a child, she had also once locked her in a suit case whilst playing: "Hide and Seek" and she left her there for some time, hence the guilt, which was compounded once she realised she had caused her sister harm in the form of a phobia.

I myself am an identical twin, so I can relate to this client, therefore I was a great help to her, and both sisters achieved successes from their sessions.

Dear student, remember close to the beginning of this chapter when you read: "Some clients will even create a false memory of the cause, to try and understand their emotions, in an attempt to relieve their fear, but that just creates more confusion and long-term, more fear as a result." Well I bring that to your attention again because this is an example of a real client that did create a false memory.

A female adult client came to me for fear of mice. She was convinced she had a phobia about them. In the pre-talk, once again using my version of free association, it came to light that as a child she lived on a farm. In the barn at the farm were hundreds of mice, and this never bothered her as a child because they would run away once she had entered the barn building, so she realised that they were more fearful of her than she could ever be of them.

As time moved on and she became a teenager, she would baby sit for a neighbour at a near-by farm and in the lounge, mice would run out of the fireplace. She would then bang her feet on the floor and they would run back into the holes they came out of. None of that ever bothered her, so I realised that this client could not possible be fearful of mice, even as an adult. However a startled response must have occurred at some point, to create a confused association of fear to mice, which could not have been a conditioned phobia, because no one else she knew had the phobia. This is what she told me had happened as the event-cause, so this was not a repressed memory. She told me that as a teenager, she was out playing with her brother and he had put a mouse in her pocket. Even though she had been brought up with seeing mice, they had never bothered her because they always ran away from her when she was present. But the thought of having to take one out of her pocket frightened her, because she would have to touch it. Realising a mouse was in her pocket caused the startled response, because she was not expecting it, so hence the association to fear of mice in the form of a phobia was created. This seems to make sense even though she had previously not feared mice, because she had never had to touch one before. There is a huge difference between expecting to see mice, so hence no startled response of fear, to then having to touch one to remove it from her pocket, which was fearful to her due to the unwanted surprise. Once the association to fear is created from the startled response within her mind, and associated to a mouse (anchor), her subconscious then does not distinguish the difference between seeing a mouse and touching one, so both the thought of seeing or touching a mouse is now fearful to her. Contradictory to the feared anchor, she had been talking about mice without showing any signs of a phobic response and that simply does not happen. So something else was going on here.

Remember that the client is placed into a light trance over time in the session, and this opens up her subconscious to release a repressed memory, and so as a result, after further talking to the client and running through the memory of the mouse in her pocket, it emerged that her brother had not placed a mouse in her pocket, it had been in fact, a worm. This client had created a false memory of the mouse in her pocket, and she had done that because the worm memory had been repressed, and so she needed something to be consciously aware of in order to try and understand her fear in an attempt to relieve the fear. But that just created more confusion and long-term more fear as a result. Also because mice were a daily occurrence around the farm, she had assumed that it must have been a mouse in her pocket, because her mind was used to seeing mice and therefore with the false memory she remembers a mouse. She had imagined the mouse and her will (conscious mind) and imagination (subconscious) were in conflict, and as you know the imagination always wins, so hence a false memory was created of trying to understand the fear that produced the phobia. Even though the memory of the mouse was false, the startled response of fear was real that she wrongly associated to a mouse. Once the client became aware of this and I had educated her on the mind, she realised that she was never scared of mice and the problem was gone.

Dear student, I know what you may be thinking. You may think that she must now have a phobia of worms. Well no, because she never had an association of fear to worms, and now as an adult she has rationalised her fear of mice as being an error, which removes the fear. The fear was never associated to worms and has not been reassociated to worms. The fear was eliminated within the session with me. Again another fascinating case, I'm sure you agree, but once again simple, once you understand what I have been teaching you.

One client was terrified of heights, and once again using my version of free association, I discovered that as a child her mother and father had taken her to the top of Blackpool Tower. Once there, her father picked her up and lifted her on top of the safety barrier, so that the only thing stopping her from falling to her death, was her father's grip on her. Due to not expecting this to happen, a startled response phobia was created with the associated emotion of fear to the anchor of heights. Her mother was a weak person, as described by the client, and she feared the child's father, and even though the mother knew the father was in the wrong, and that her daughter was petrified, she did not stop him. This was clearly a form a child abuse from the father, as it gave him sadistic pleasure, a sense of control, and it gave him a deluded sense of feeling powerful. Therefore, I made the client see him for his true nature, so that she realised she was and is in the right, and had been from the beginning. The relationship between them was bad. I had not shown the client something that she did not already know. Her conscious mind knew, but her subconscious was playing a different movie of it all being her fault. Victims tend to blame themselves for the abuse that they suffer, because the abuser conditions into the victim's impressionable mind that it is their fault. For example, the abuser says: "Look what you made me do" when harming the victim. Once the memory was known, I used timeline and took her back in time as the adult she now is, to comfort the child she once was, because that is what she needed as a child, because she had received no comfort from anyone as a child with her fear. Another happy client was achieved due to her now understanding her fear and rationalise it through the mind of an adult, which removes the old childlike view and emotions from her past problem.

I received an email from a young businessman, who believed he lacked confidence when talking to people on the phone at work. Hence why he emailed me from his place of work and didn't phone. He also wanted a confidence building session due to feeling extreme anxiety once a phone started to ring at work in the office. If he answered it then he would get to a point where his mouth would go dry and he had a feeling of vomiting, he was then unable to speak to the caller. This of course is the: "Fright Response" and previous to a session with me he did not know that, so, due to lack of understanding of his problem and mind, this had made matters worse for him. People start to feel that they are going mad, when in fact it is a normal reaction, once the phobia is present within a person's subconscious mind. He told me that even before a phone would ring in the office, he knew that he would be anxious once it had, and this thought process of course is his imagination, and his anxiety reaction was his subconscious, warning him of possible danger due to the negative habit that he created, even though no danger was present. □

Remember that the mind delivers what we focus on. He was playing a negative movie within his subconscious and so that was the result, once faced in the same situation in real life. This client had created a phobia of phone calls in the work place that started from an initial event-cause of fear that he wrongly associated to a phone. He was repeatedly playing a negative scenario in his mind of bad feelings before and during a phone call, hence the anxiety of fright response. This was a recent development that only happened at work, so I knew that this was not a phobia that had been conditioned into him as a child. I also knew that it could not have been conditioned into him from others recently, because for that to happen, someone at his works would have to have the same phobia and be around him for long periods each day, in order to condition the fear of phone calls and talking on the phone into him. In an office environment the odds of that happening are close to zero, so that was highly unlikely to have been the cause. So the phobia must have been caused by a startled response at work, hence the association of bad feeling towards talking on the phone at work and no other place.

Also because I understand the mind, I knew for a fact that the initial cause of the phobia was an emotional fear that he already felt before he answered a phone call, so the fear was reassociated to the anchor of the phone call. Any phobic response after that, was just a habit of a reactivated anchor, and therefore his subconscious warning of a danger that was not real. So like all phobic's he unknowingly was not fearful of what he came to therapy for. The emotional, fearful event-cause was something else that he then reassociated the fear from to the thought of talking on and hearing the phone ring in the office. The fact he did not fear phones at home proves his fear in the office of phones was not a genuine fear; it was just an irrational phobia.

By using free association from one related memory to another via my questions, I was able to find the earliest situation that he had remembered where he felt anxiety at work. This remembered event was not previously repressed and it was not in relation to a phone call at all. It was at work in a boardroom meeting of ten people and he felt anxiety before entering the meeting. Considering he felt extreme anxiety and fear before that meeting, I knew that this was not the source (event-cause) of the startled response phobia. I also knew it wasn't the cause because it was not a previous repressed memory, because I knew that the cause was repressed because the client did not know why he was having phobic response to a phone in the office. With this new information, I was getting closer to the cause, and remember that when a client tells you the first memory that they can remember of feeling anxiety or a phobic response, that memory is never the event-cause you are looking for, because the effect is already present, and the cause is a repressed memory, so of course the client cannot tell you the real event-cause memory yet.

Therefore the cause of the phobia must have been from a previous meeting to the one he told me and my thoughts were proven to be right. This is because, with my free association questions, I had eliminated all other causes. For example: Was he stressed before entering work? Or had he been told some bad news before entering work? Or had he had an argument with someone? I was looking for an event that caused the fear, the source of the problem that he had reassociated to phones in the office within his subconscious, and the only event that was left was a previous meeting at work from the one he told me about. This is what had happened. He was new to the job and it was the first time his boss had taken him into a boardroom meeting. We all feel a sense of nervousness in a new situation. This is natural because it's the mind's way of protecting us against a potential danger, even though one is not present. It is fear of the unknown, being cautious, and that is normal. During the meeting his boss suddenly, without warning, asked my client: "What are your thoughts on the subject of expanding the growth of the business as discussed?" This of course startled my client, because he was not prepared for the question, and having already felt nervous, this startled response developed into fear, in which he then wrongly associated with work phone calls. So all that nervousness of a new job, combined to the fear of his first time in a meeting, and then being put on the spot by the question, with not knowing how to answer; all this combination of built up anxiety and the startled response, generated overwhelming, emotional fear and that fear had to go somewhere.

Remember the: "Flight, Fight or Flight Response chapter" in the Volume One Book? This client could not: "Fight or Flight" in his situation, so how was all that emotion released? Well it wasn't. And that is the problem, so his mind couldn't handle it (kettle effect), so it represses the memory and reassociates the emotion to the next thing he hears. Hence a phobia of phones at work is created, with the phone ringing being the anchor. Basically an emotion of fear was generated within him, and then he reassociated that emotion to the thought of a phone call, due to hearing a phone ring, and at the same time the memory that created the emotion was repressed, due to what his mind considered to be traumatic, but the association of fear to a phone call was remembered.

Dear student, I trust that you understand how I found the cause of the effect he was suffering from. It is so easy to take psychotherapy skills for granted, by thinking why do people not work this out for themselves, because it is so logical to me, but the fact is, people don't have a clue about understanding their own mind or situation. The questions asked to a client are very relevant in investigating (free associating) the clients problem, but yet they don't make the connection as to why I am asking the questions until I later explain. That lack of knowledge and understanding on their part is fantastic for me, the therapist, because it creates confusion in their mind because they are trying to find an understanding to the relevance of the line of questioning. This of course is a "Trans-Derivational Search (TDS)" which bypasses the conscious mind and opens up the subconscious, which releases the repressed memory via light trance that is coaxed out by use of the correct questions and skills by me the therapist. I love my job.

In the hypnosis part of the session, after creating a good feeling anchor, I then ran the scenario of him answering the phone at work, and the caller having a comical, squeaky voice. This made it humorous and I also added that the caller was breaking wind and burping. I did this due to the client telling me in the pre-talk that he would find that funny after I suggested the idea to him. I also talked him though an imagined boardroom meeting with all his work colleagues being naked and again breaking wind and burping. The old associations of fear changed for the new, comical ones, and the session was very successful.

Dear student, remember that the more ridiculous, childlike and comical you make the new scenario of an old situation, the more success the client will have. The humorous, good feelings of emotions are then reassociated to that previous situation of talking on the phone at work. Hence the old negative associations have gone, and also within all future work meetings. You will now appreciate that, the power of hypnosis and the correct way of approaching and phrasing verbal speech, is very skilful in reprogramming negative thought patterns. Other phobias can all be dealt with in a similar manner for a lasting cure. Also if the client naturally abreacts, simply reassure them with the good feeling anchor that you have created. The abreaction means they will then have offloaded the emotion of a past event, which had caused them indirectly to be scared of spiders, water or whatever the phobia was.

Most of the time people are not aware of what a phobia really is until I point it out to them. As with the last example, the client thought he lacked confidence, when in fact he had a simple phobia. Of course he didn't lack confidence because he got the job. Plus I knew it could not have been a lack of confidence because he had answered the phone confidently thousands of times previously to the phobia developing. Phobias are extremely easy to overcome, due to the fear being a reassociation and not a fear of what they think they fear. Educate the client on the mind and what a phobia is, and instruct the client to imagine that what they once feared is now a humorous situation, and allow the client to ridicule whatever it was they once had a phobic response to. This makes the client see a funny side to their past problem, and therefore changes the associations towards it. Then in the future, after the session, when they are confronted by the same situation that they once had a phobic response to, they now have a pleasant feeling.

Make the cognitive subconscious image so ridiculous that the client will remember it, for example: a client that fears any insect or animal is to, within their subconscious mind under hypnosis, dress up the feared insect or animal in the most ridiculously funny clothes. This eliminates the past fear, as they now find it pleasurably funny. I will explain more on this later as we continue.

Start here. Fear Phobia Pre-talk

What follows is the Pre-talk to the hypnotic induction. This script can be adapted and used for any phobia or fear, but as an example I have used spiders. I have written both the pre-talk and what is said under hypnosis, far longer than it needs be. I have done this purposely, to give you more examples of what can be said and so that you can pick and choose what you may feel fits that particular client best. So, in short, this script is not intended to be read word for word to the client. It can even be used in a number of sessions if needed, to make them different from the previous, and please remember to always personalise a session to the client.

I always start by asking the client about their problem and situation to gain the information needed for the session. This time also allows me the time needed to build rapport. I then ask: "Do you agree that there are two parts of the human mind, the conscious mind (their conscious will) and the subconscious mind (their imagination)?" All would tend to agree with that there are two parts.

Please note, I never mention the third part of the mind, the analytical area of the mind to a client, because they do not need that information. So keep it simple. I only gave that information to you because you are my student, and of course, you are not training a student, they are a client, so the two parts of the mind is all they need to know.

I then ask the client: "Which part of the mind is in control of what you will be doing day-to-day?" And 99% of the time, clients will say: "The conscious mind." This is for two reasons: firstly, most people think they are consciously in control, and secondly, I also lead the client in the direction of saying: "Conscious Mind."

Dear student, how do I lead a client to say: "Conscious mind and why"? Think about that question, because the answer you have already been taught and therefore you know, even if you think you don't know.

This is what I do. I ask: "Do you agree that there are two parts of the mind, the conscious mind and the subconscious mind?" When I say: "Conscious mind," I lift my left hand, and by doing so I have created an anchor within the client's mind of the thought of: "Conscious Mind" being associated to my left hand, which is the anchor. I then put my left hand down and then when saying: "Subconscious Mind," I raise my right hand, and therefore by doing so I have created an anchor (right hand) associated to the words and thought of the: "Subconscious Mind" and then I put my right hand down. I then ask the client: "Which part of the mind is in control of what you will be doing day-to-day?" At the same time of asking that question, I reactivate the anchor with the association of thinking of the: "Conscious Mind" by simply raising my left hand, and so the client is led to answer the question by saying: "Conscious Mind" and then I put my left hand down. I then tell the client: "You are in fact wrong. It is the subconscious mind (reinforce the anchor by raising the right hand) that is in control and I will explain why later in the session" (then drop the right hand). I then reassure them that everyone gets it wrong and that avoids any confrontation and prevents the client from feeling foolish.

Dear student, can you think of why I have done that? Why had I led the client to think and say: "Conscious Mind" when it is wrong? How do I benefit from this as a therapist? Well I benefit in five ways as follows:

First benefit, I now know the client can be led, and therefore they are suggestible, which makes the session easy.

Second benefit, I also created a third anchor, can you work out what the third anchor is? It is not an obvious one, so I wouldn't expect even an experience therapist to figure out what I have done. I'll give you a hint. The first anchor was my left hand associated to thinking of and therefore saying the: "Conscious Mind." The second anchor was my right hand associated to the thought of the: "Subconscious Mind" and the third anchor was created once I said: "You are in fact wrong, it is the subconscious mind." It was at this point that the third anchor was created when I reinforced the second anchor by raising the right hand.

Even though I have given you that information, I still wouldn't expect you to have worked out what the third anchor is or what it is for, if you have, then well done you. When I lifted my right hand a second time I was reinforcing the second anchor to the thought of the subconscious mind. However because at that point I had made the client aware that the subconscious was the right answer, I had also then quickly changed the second anchor (right hand) to now thinking it's right (correct answer). So now the second anchor's association has been changed from thinking of the subconscious mind to realising it is right, it is the correct answer. Once the new association to the anchor (right hand) was created, I put my right hand down, so that the associated link to being right remained to be used again later in the session.

So I can class this as a new second anchor or third anchor with the original association to the second anchor having now been replaced. Remember the subconscious can only ever remember the last thing that was associated to an anchor. In this case the new thought of knowing it is right (correct answer) to the anchor of the right hand. The original association to the second anchor was: "Subconscious Mind" but that association had served its purpose and was no longer needed, so I replaced it for the added benefit of leading the client to associate the right hand to represent the right answer, the correct answer, which implies the right thing to do. I can use this anchor later in the session when I want to provoke, or lead the client to the right answer to whatever future question I ask them. Notice that I use the right hand for the right answer and not the left, hence why: "Conscious Mind" association was left hand, as it was the wrong answer. If I had made the right hand as the anchor for the wrong answer, then it would not have had the same use, and it would have been confusing for the client due to the word: "Right" hand being used for wrong and not right. Always use right hand anchor for a leading signal for the right answer or right thing to do, as in my opinion it should be. I will be using this signal anchor later in the script.

Third benefit of leading the client to say: "Conscious Mind" is the creation of a "Trans-Derivational Search (TDS)" within their mind by me replying with saying: "You are in fact wrong, it is the subconscious mind that is in control and I will explain why later in the session." By saying that I created a: "Trans-Derivational Search (TDS)" within the client's mind because they are now consciously wondering how could they be wrong. How can it be the subconscious that is in control, and I wonder how he is going to explain this? This sent the conscious mind on a journey and therefore bypassed via TDS, which opens up their subconscious to suggestion, which cements the anchor of right hand meaning right answer, the right thing to do.

Fourth benefit is that the client's subconscious knows I am in control. When a client is led to answer wrongly, they accept that they were wrong because I proved to them, with my knowledge that I am right. The client knows that I am right, and so they will agree to all future suggestions and commands from me as being right. I have become the authority figure of reason, truth and knowing what is right. My knowledge gains the clients trust in me. This way I avoid confrontation within the session because the client knows I must be right throughout, regardless of any opposing ideas they may have previously had.

Fifth benefit is that the client is now in light trance due to the TDS and rapport built.

I continue by asking for information about the client, that way I can personalise the session to suit them. I could ask what have they tried in the past, and what their routine is at the moment. I personalise the pre-talk based on the information the client provides.
I ask:

1) What methods have you tried to overcome your phobia?
2) Have you had any success with any of those?
3) What's the most important reason for you to overcome this phobia? (This may give me a good feeling anchor to use later).
4) Talk me through the last event that led up to your first phobic reaction?
5) Tell me about a happy time in your life but if you cannot think of one straight away than imagine a time when you would feel like that? (Finding a good feeling anchor again).
6) What are your ambitions in life? (Finding a good feeling anchor again).
7) Tell me about a time when you felt comfortable, warm, and happy and secure, a time in your life when you were relaxed, warm and comfortable in a quiet place. (Finding a good feeling anchor again and of course generating a good relaxing feeling to use in the hypnosis induction).
8) Tell me about the first time you can remember when you had a phobic response (whatever it may be). Run me through the scene from start to finish.
9) Tell me a song or a tune that makes you laugh. It could be from your childhood like the Muppet Show, something like that. (This can be

used later in the session as a good feeling anchor.) If not a song, then a situation or person or a character from a movie may be.

☐

Dear student, also ask more free association questions to find the event-cause of the phobia if the cause is not already known. I have already explained free association and the questions in details. The information gathered from the above questions can be used later in the session. The more information I have on their problem, the more successful the session will be, because I can personalise the session to them. I continue the pre-talk by telling my clients: "Personalised sessions are far more successful than a group session. That's why I do not do group sessions because each individual is different and you are the only person that matters at the moment." (Saying this makes the client feel important and of course they are) then continue by educating the client by saying:

"A phobia is an excessive or unreasonable fear reaction, which is linked to an object, place or situation. Phobias are extremely common. A phobia can develop through a conditioned, learned response from a family member or friend. For example: if your parents were scared of dogs, then as a child it is conditioned into you to fear dogs so hence a phobia is born. Even so, most phobias develop after an incident which created a startled response and an emotional reaction of fear. Then our subconscious wrongly associates that fear to an object, place or situation. To understand what a phobia is and how most develop, it is first very important that you understand what a: "Startled Response" is. Because it explains how some phobias began in the first place, and in order to deal with a problem you must first understand it. This is just one of many examples of how a phobia can develop. I will use spiders as an example. If there is a sudden unexpected movement then everyone will jump because the body and mind focuses towards this new stimulus. So even the biggest fan of spiders would jump if a spider startled them. It is a normal, human response of the: "Fright, Fight or Flight Responses."

"However, a person that accepts spiders would quickly calm down after with the thought: "Oh it's only a spider, I'm safe" and they would then laugh it off. But if you were already partially stressed by something totally unrelated to a spider, like work or life in general, and then startled by a spider, the stress you already had would overflow, adding to the startled response with a feeling of fear. Then in your mind, the spider becomes associated with feelings of feared panic. When in fact, you were already stressed before you saw the spider, but the startled response added to the stress you already had. So the combination of the stress that is now present adds to more stress and therefore feared panic. Basically the stress you already had is reassociated to the spider (anchor) caused by the startled response."

Dear student, notice how I am repeating myself there so that there can be no misunderstanding within the client's mind of what I am explaining. Let us continue.

If the startled response was intense enough, your subconscious mind wrongly associates spiders to the feeling of fear. So that in the future, when you see a spider, your subconscious again wrongly associates this fear to the spider, due to the memory of the connection you wrongly created between the spider (anchor) and fear (emotional association), hence a phobia is born. The spider becomes an associated anchor to the feelings of fear, so when you next see a spider, which is the anchor, it triggers the associated emotion of fear.

This is similar to a song you once heard which you automatically associate emotional feelings to from a past situation you were in, so that in the future, when you hear the song, that anchor triggers the emotions that you have previously associated to it, as if you were back in that place where you first heard the song. This is because the human mind works by association. When we experience two things together for a little while, one will automatically remind us of the other in the future. So when you are in a situation that you felt fear in the past, that associated emotion to the anchor (your phobia), signals to your subconscious mind to make you feel bad again, as if it is doing you a favour warning you, and protecting you from danger, even though none maybe present, and most of the time with phobic's there is in fact no danger, because the fear is irrational.

It is the associated emotion that we need to change later in the session, by making a new, positive association to replace the old association to the same anchor. In this example the anchor being a spider, but in your case the anchor (is whatever the client came to overcome fear of). Basically most phobias are your mind wrongly identifying a startled response as a threat, when in fact it is not or need not be, and other phobias are conditioned into a person from other people with the same phobia. With the help of hypnosis you will begin to relax around the idea of spiders (or whatever the clients phobia was), then the old artificial association disconnects, leaving you free from the fear of spiders permanently or whatever your fear or phobia was.

The only reason you think you have a fear or phobia is because you know what happened the last time you saw the object, or you were in a place or situation with the association of fear that you created. But that will never happen again after a session with me, because you will become aware of your own mind and responses and you will have the ability to control your thoughts. When a person with a phobia is in or even anticipates being in the situation that they once felt the phobia, they experience immediate anxiety. The physical symptoms of anxiety may include: increased heart rate (palpitations), shortness of breath, sweating, tight chest, and shaking. They also feel an intense fear of losing control, being embarrassed, fainting or feeling sick. Our thought processes can actually make the phobic response worse, because we often think about the situation and how it makes us feel before it happens. We imagine in our minds how terrible the event will be and usually see ourselves messing up. If you say to yourself: "Don't think of a spider" then you will think of one, making the situation worse than it need be. It would be far better to think of something that you find pleasurable, instead of thinking about what you don't want. You see you are what you think. An example of these thought processes would be, when you would like to approach someone in a bar for instance, to get know them. If you are anxious about this, then you will often play the scenario in your mind first. It usually goes something like this: oh he/she is gorgeous, I would like to get to know them better, but they are too good for me, look how good they look. They will probably laugh if I asked for a dance. I bet all his/her mates would laugh too. Then the rest of the pub would laugh or look at me. You then imagine this happening. Such is the power of our imagination that this stops you from doing your conscious thought of approaching the person. It is the same with phobias, because the cause can be explained more as a conditioned (habit learned) anxiety response through repetition, and the cause brought on by an initial startled response, which has become associated with the feared object, place or situation. Our subconscious mind associates these feelings with the situations, even if it is imagined.

Phobia or Confidence Mind Model

Dear student, this mind model sub-chapter is for phobias, and can also be adapted for clients with low confidence problems. The following is said to the client:

The mind is split up into two parts. You have the conscious and the subconscious parts of the mind. At the beginning of this session you thought that you were consciously in control of your life, however as we continue you will realise that the conscious is the part of the mind that we would like to think is in control, but it is not, it is the subconscious mind that is in control.

For example: you do not think about breathing, blood circulation, making your heart beat, because the subconscious is the autopilot for the body, it is running the body twenty four hours a day, seven days a week. The subconscious part of the mind can do many things at a time and whilst it is running the body, it is also taking in two million pieces of information every second, passing on what it thinks is important to the conscious mind and disregarding the rest. For example: you buy a new car and you are driving down the road in your new car, now it seems like every other car is the same as yours, and they are even the same colour. Even though you cannot remember seeing so many of these same cars the day before. So did everyone go and buy the identical type of new car at the same time as you? No, of course not. The day before, the subconscious still noticed all these cars, but it thought that type of car was not important to you, so the subconscious did not pass the information on to the conscious mind. Therefore you were not fully aware of them even though they were there. But now you have got this new car, it has got to be important to you, because you first imagined buying and driving the car and then consciously did what you first subconsciously imagined. Because in order to do anything in life, we have first got to imagine doing it. So because you imagined it and then did it, the subconscious realises this type of car is now important to you, and so now it passes the information on every time it sees this type of car, so you are now consciously aware of seeing more of those cars than you have ever seen in your life.

You see, the two parts of the mind have become friends where the thought of this car is concerned. That is what you have not done with your phobia or low confidence problem, you have never imagined seeing yourself overcome this past problem, so there is still conflict with the conscious and subconscious mind, and when the will and imagination are in conflict, the imagination always wins, due to the subconscious being the more powerful.

You see, you have made a conscious decision to overcome the phobia or low confidence problem, but you have not been able to, because you tried to solve your problem on a conscious level, but your problem is within your subconscious mind and not your conscious one. Let me explain.

The conscious part of the mind is very logical and very rational. It is the part that you use when making your decisions on a day to day basis. But it is the imagination (subconscious) that determines whether we carry out those conscious decisions or not. Last week you may have made the conscious decision to go swimming, but then you imagined that the water was cold. How do you know? Because you did not go swimming, that imagined thought stopped you doing something, you had made a conscious decision to do. Therefore your subconscious mind is in control. This is what has happened with your phobia (anxiety, low confidence) problem. You consciously want to overcome that phobia (anxiety, low confidence) but you are still playing a different movie in your subconscious imagination. Again conflict is at work, so you will never win when only trying to overcome a problem consciously. The conscious is the part where your willpower is held, but of course, you have got to remember to use it. I know you can use it because you had the will to get up this morning, wash and clothe yourself, and you have had the will power to come here for therapy. So we know it is there.

The conscious part of your mind can think of only one thought or idea at once. This is why we can only concentrate on doing one task at a time when doing it consciously. However, we can do many tasks, but only one is conscious, and the others are subconscious, in the form of a habit, whether they are good or bad habits. The conscious mind is a very slow part of the mind. And this is why we get stressed out. We try to do too many things at the same time consciously and that part of the mind cannot do it. You know what happens: the phone rings, someone wants your attention and you are trying to cook the evening meal, you are stressed out because you try to do all three things at once. Take a step back, realise what is happening and do one task at a time. Doing one task does not get us stressed. Trying to do two tasks consciously starts the stress ball rolling. It is like a snowball rolling down a hill, the more tasks you try to do at once, the more the stress builds up, and once we get stressed out, we are now not able to do any of the tasks we were trying to do. Stop, take a step back in your mind and realise what is happening and why you are stressed and simply do one task at a time. That way you have a better chance of carrying out the entire task.

This stress build up makes your phobic or low confidence response even worse once confronted by the same situation, the anchor that triggers off the associated emotion to fear where you had a phobic response or low confidence previously. Then, over time, several phobic or low confidence feelings later, the subconscious part of the mind thinks: "I can do that job for you" and it took your problem on as a habit to free up your conscious mind's burden, so the subconscious thinks it is doing you a favour. Because all a habit is, is something you do consciously a number of times and then the subconscious will take it on as a habit. So trying to change it consciously is impossible, because the problem is now subconscious.

The subconscious part of the mind knows that you can only consciously concentrate on doing one task at a time, so the more jobs the subconscious can do on your behalf the better. As far as the subconscious is concerned, it is doing you a favour by taking on the problem as a habit, because also, the subconscious does not know it is a problem, it is just a habit that you want to do as far as your subconscious is concerned. It will keep the habit until you subconsciously remove the habit, by changing the negative associated link to a positive one, so that you feel comfortable about what was once unnecessarily fearful. And we will do that via hypnosis later. Driving is another habit. Again, when you first started to learn to drive you drove consciously, you had to think about mirror, signal, brakes, clutch, and what is going on around you. It was impossible to have a conversation because your conscious mind was occupied on the one task of driving, and that part of the mind can only do one task at once. But you passed your test and practiced and now you do not even have to consciously think about driving, because your subconscious has taken the task on as a habit, in order to free up your conscious minds burden. Now when driving down the road if someone pulls out in front of you, you just stop automatically, because you do not have to consciously think about driving. When you drive home from work, before you know it you are home and cannot consciously remember the details of most of the journey you have just had. You know the journey you have taken, because you take the same journey every day, so your subconscious has taken on driving that route as a habit, and so you subconsciously drove home, hence why you cannot consciously remember the full journey. That is called: "Highway Hypnosis." So hypnosis comes naturally to you. Your life is full of habits, for example: swimming is a habit, riding a bike, reading, walking, the way you brush your teeth, because you no longer need to give those tasks any conscious thought.

Our lives are full of habits, because a habit is only something you do consciously a number of times, which is then taken on by the subconscious as a habit, regardless of whether the habit is good for you or not.

Now, at the moment, the subconscious is protecting these habits. It does not want you to forget to drive as you drive down the road. It does not want you to forget to swim whilst swimming across a river. It is also protecting the habit of your phobia, anxiety or low confidence, because the subconscious does not know the difference between a good or bad habit. A habit is a habit through repetition as far as the subconscious is concerned. So it is still running the old emotions with the same reaction response of anxiety in the form of a habit. It is still running the same old movie of something it thinks you want to do and how it thinks you want to emotionally feel, so you are fighting between the two parts of your mind, because you want to consciously change, but you haven't told your subconscious that. There is the problem.

Your conscious knows all the reasons why you want to overcome your problem, but the subconscious is still rerunning the old reasons of associated fear of why you started the problem in the first place.

The subconscious holds all your memories and emotions. You have got memories stored within your subconscious going all the way back to childhood, but you cannot consciously always recall them. Then a song might come on the radio and all of a sudden you can remember a memory that you have associated to that song, who you were with, what you were doing, even what you were wearing in that past time, and you feel the emotions that you previously associated to that song. This is an associated link. When we experience two things together for a little while, one will automatically remind us of the other in the future. In the subconscious are your emotions and emotions are controlled by the subconscious, so due to the habit, you feel phobic, anxiety, low confidence, once that negative associated emotion has been triggered via the reactivated anchor.

Another reason you have not been able to overcome your past problem is due to lack of understanding of it and lack of understanding of your own mind and the responses you have been suffering from. Also your imagination is in the subconscious, and the imagination is very powerful. For example: you have probably had dreams or nightmares before and you have woken up shaking, sweating and your heart pounding, but yet you have not been anywhere, you are still in bed. Well this is because the subconscious part of the mind does not know the difference between something real or imagined, both are your reality. So if you are having a dream of running down the road scared, as far as the subconscious is concerned it is actually happening, therefore it makes physical, organic changes to the body, hence you wake up shaking, sweating and your heart pounding.

The problem is that a lot of the time when you try to overcome a fear you are consciously saying to yourself: "I am not scared of spiders" (or whatever it may be). Well what are you imagining when you say that? Yes that is right, you are imagining and saying to yourself: "Fear of spiders," so you are getting the subconscious to imagine a spider, making it challenging for you to overcome the fear because the subconscious knows it has always associated spiders to fear. So when you imagine one, or see one, you have implanted a powerful suggestion that sets of an alarm in your head to remind you to feel the fear. The subconscious is reminding you to do something that it thinks you still want to do, and that is to feel fear when a spider is around or just by thinking about a spider (or whatever their problem is).

Remember that the subconscious mind does not know the difference between what is real or imagined, so just by imagining a spider you feel real fear. Imagination (subconscious) always overpowers knowledge within your conscious, so you consciously want to overcome the problem, but your imagination within your subconscious is still playing the same negative movie in the form of a habit, that the subconscious does not know is causing you emotional harm.

Now what you have got to do is imagine it is going to be easy for you to overcome the phobia and make it humorous. You have got associated connections with certain activities. For example: going on holiday to a hot country and seeing more spiders and certain times when you regularly see them. Now, by imagining those situations with a humorous spider, as a fun friend, is what we need to do today on a subconscious level, because that is where the problem is.

So the next time you see a spider the subconscious just makes it easy for you. This is because you have already imagined what is going to happen when you see another, and so the subconscious will just make it easy for you because you have associated the spider to a humorous thought. A new, improved associated emotion, instead of fear. The subconscious mind can only associate one emotion to an anchor, so we are going to change it from the neurological pain of fear, to pleasure. You see you have been telling yourself on a conscious level that you want to overcome your fear, but you have not been able to, because fear is associated within your subconscious mind to the situation of seeing a spider (or whatever the client's problem is). It has become a negative habit and therefore positivity has not been passed on to your subconscious mind to override the fear. You are consciously aware of negativity, due to still playing the negative movie within the subconscious.

So you have not been able to overcome the problem, because when the conscious will and subconscious imagination are in conflict, the imagination will always win, because it is the more powerful part of the mind. You have been going about it all wrong on a conscious level and this is where I come in, to help you on a subconscious level, through hypnosis.

So that is what you do in a session with me, you use the imagination under hypnosis to overcome the problem. For example: if you consciously think, do not think of a black cat, you have then imagined a black cat, making it impossible to stop imagining the cat. What you consciously wanted to achieve: "Do not think of a black cat" has had the opposite effect on the subconscious mind, and so you focus on the cat instead of something else to overcome the thought of the black cat. You have gone about your problem consciously and it has had the opposite effect. So again this is where hypnosis comes in, there is no magic trick or waving of a magic wand with hypnosis. It is a way of getting you to relax, and because you are relaxed I can talk directly to your subconscious, the part that is in control. Because I am talking to the subconscious, together we can rerecord an up-to-date movie, so that your past irrational problem becomes humorous and it is something you now feel comfortable about. I am only helping you to do something in which you already want to do, but in the past you have not known how. So we are taking away the old associated emotions to the bad habit, and replacing it with the new emotion of feeling good in that situation that you once felt bad. After the session you will feel great because you have both parts of the mind working as one, to keep you from feeling how you felt in the past.

As I have mentioned, the primary function of the subconscious is to protect habits, and by doing so it thinks it is protecting you. We know this because if pulled under the water when swimming, you automatically go to the surface and subconsciously swim, due to the protected habit of swimming in order to protect you from the danger of drowning. Your subconscious has also done the same with your problem, it has protected the habit because it thinks it is doing you a favour, just the same as protecting the habit of swimming. This is because your subconscious doesn't know the difference between a good or bad habit, and so the subconscious protects the habit regardless of the type of habit, even if it is harming you cognitively because it does not know that it is. You never told the subconscious, you only told the conscious, and the subconscious won the battle. So with my help using hypnosis, we will now replace and therefore remove the past associated emotions of fear and the old movie that was a conditioned habit of feeling nervous as you no longer need it. Then your subconscious will keep you free from those negative thoughts again, as you take on a new, positive associated emotion of thinking, or seeing spiders, or where ever you felt low confidence. So with hypnosis we are going to replace the old habit with a new positive move and emotion. We are going to get you to use the imagination to imagine it is easy, and then it will be, because it is, and by doing so we are going to remind the subconscious that it has got to protect the new, healthy ways of thinking and the positive new habit.

Dear student, basically explain the mind model to the client and cover the four reference points of the mind, and the seven mind rules were appropriate to their problem. There is one more thing to add to your script, with regards to the mind model. That is, the subconscious mind has no concept of time, so it will be easy to overcome the client's problem. You could say to your client:

"You see the human mind works by association. When we experience two things together for a little while, one (the anchor), will automatically remind us of the other (associated memory and emotions), in the future. That is also proof that the subconscious mind has no concept of time. Remember the subconscious mind reference point (C): "The subconscious mind has no concept of time, past, present or future." The associated links of memory and emotions to the anchor, will be the same age twenty years from now, the same age from the day you created the anchor, so you will still remember the event and (or just), feel those same emotions that you have associated to the song, as if you were back in that time, the day you created the anchor. This is due to the subconscious mind not realising that twenty years have gone by, it is as if it were yesterday. Your physical body has aged, but those associated links to the anchor, are the same age as the day they were created, and therefore the subconscious mind has no concept of time. This means that memories and emotions within the subconscious do not age, and also a memory and emotion are two separate things from the same event, hence why a memory can be repressed and the emotion be remembered. Why the memory can be repressed was explained in my Beginners to Advanced Volume One Book. Of course you consciously know past, present and future, but that is not where the associated links to the anchor are stored. A memory, emotion (associated links to an anchor), are stored within the subconscious. Even though a memory and emotion cannot be changed and are the same age throughout life, we can still create a new memory and emotion of the same event to the same anchor, in order to replace the old, via the subconscious, using hypnosis. This way we rationalise an event through an adult's perspective, instead of the child's old perspective, so that any negative effect that the associations to an anchor were causing, can be removed and replaced for new positive associations."

Dear student. In this script I am simply showing another way of explaining the information to make it more personal to the client's problem. Reading this script of ideas, you will realise that what the client is told, and what I have taught you to do as a therapist, the skills, the understanding of the client's problem and the way they think, and how I advise of how you need to think are two very different mindsets. The therapist is using skills that the client is not consciously aware of, tone of voice, observation, building rapport, leading, etc. They do not know techniques like free association or the fact that you are bypassing their conscious mind via a TDS; they don't need to know your skills. As long as the client understands what you are saying, they don't need to know the real reason you say certain things, or your body language like the manipulation anchor at the beginning of this script to get the client to say: "Conscious Mind." That skill used both verbal and non-verbal manipulation that the client is not aware of consciously. All they need to know is the understanding of their problem, how to solve the problem and understanding their own mind. What the therapist is doing in the back ground is a skill the client will never be fully conscious of. You the therapist are in fact controlling two minds very differently, yours and the clients and yours will be always one step ahead of the clients, because you have the psychotherapy skill knowledge that they don't. So there is no need to fully explain what you are in fact doing to the client, just make sure that what you are doing works.

What Do You Know About Hypnosis?

Dear student, only say the following if the client is worried about being hypnotised, because the more they understand, the more they will relax around the idea of being hypnotised, because their negative worrying preconceptions are wrong. Continue:

Well, I cannot make you do anything that you do not want to do. This surprises some people because they see those hypnosis shows on the TV and it does make it look like they are making people do what they do not want to. Think about it, why do people go to see those shows? They go to be entertained, to see people act stupid. So then, they ask for a volunteer. Now who is going to volunteer? So the hypnotist entertainer has all these people on stage and he starts deciding who will be the most entertaining, who is the biggest show off. The people in the audience might be thinking that he is looking for people that are hypnotisable, but he is not, because he knows that anyone is hypnotisable, so he is looking for the biggest show offs, the ones that want to be the centre of attention, the biggest exhibitionists. Now he has got it made, he is not making them do something they do not want to do; he is making them do what they already want to do. And that is great because that is exactly what we are doing today. I am not making you overcome your past problem; I am helping you do something you already want to do. Hypnosis is a great way for getting you to do what you already want to do but couldn't, due to trying consciously. When you relax via hypnosis you will not fall asleep, you will be aware of everything. You hear the sounds outside the room, the sounds from in the room, you remember everything. You still have thoughts running through your mind, one of those thoughts might be: "Am I hypnotised?" Well the answer to that is yes, because hypnosis is a feeling of being relaxed, and because you are relaxed, I can talk directly to the subconscious part of your mind in order to help you overcome the past problem.

The best way to describe hypnosis is to say that it feels like first thing in the morning, you have just woken up but you have not opened your eyes yet, you know you can open your eyes if you want to, but you do not want to because you are so relaxed. You are going in and out of hypnosis all day long, without even realising it. The most common form of hypnosis is driving. You are driving down the road on a trip you have done a hundred times before and you start to daydream or think about something else. Next thing you know you get to your destination and you have no idea how you got there. That is: "Highway Hypnosis." Whilst driving, your conscious mind has wandered off and your more powerful subconscious has driven you safely to your destination, due to the habit of driving the same route many times in the past. Also, reading a book or watching the TV. You are at home and you are watching TV and you are hanging on every word that is happening. Someone asks you a question and you do not hear them, or you do not want to hear them, because you are so relaxed and don't want to be disturbed.

Now there are a number of ways to respond to hypnotic suggestions. For example: you could respond within your mind by thinking: "Yes" or "No." So if I make a suggestion of: "You are now ready to overcome the past problem" and you think: "Yes I am" then that suggestion will work, and it will work every time in working towards a positive result of achieving your goal. Another way to respond is to be uncomfortable with the suggestion. For example: if I say: "You are now ready to confront your fear" and you think: "No I am not" then that suggestion I made will be rejected, so you are in control at all times. I sometimes have people in therapy who have been sent to me by their husbands, wives, or doctors, and they say: "Get in there and sort your problem out" and like I said, I cannot make someone do what they do not want to do. So again the suggestion is rejected because that type of client is unmotivated, they do not want to overcome their problem. Another way to respond is to hope. Now, there is a problem with the word hope, it is the twin sister of the word try. If I try to pick up this pen up, I do not do it because I am just trying, if I want to pick it up I will. The subconscious is too busy doing a hundred and one other things to care if you are just trying. Therefore if you are uncomfortable, unmotivated or just hoping and trying then the subconscious has not got time to listen and so will just reject any suggestions. However by being motivated and wanting change for the better, and by you agreeing and liking the suggestions I give, and by you wanting this session to work, not only will the positive suggestions be accepted, they will also be acted upon.

Hypnosis is like a contract between two people. My part of the contract is to give you all the thoughts and therapies that I know are going to make you happier. Your part of the contract is to follow along with the suggestions, want them to work and allow them to work. Now I know I am going to keep up with my part of the contract. Are you going to keep up to yours? Good, then we are going to be successful.

☐

Dear student, at this point you can do a suggestion test on the client as explained in the Volume One Book. This will prove to them how powerful the subconscious mind is, it also adds to the belief in what you have told them about the mind model. Have you noticed that the information just given in this sub-chapter contradicts what I have taught you? With regards to what is said to the client when talking about hypnosis, I wrote: "Well, I cannot make you do anything that you do not want to do." As a student you know that is nonsense, because under hypnosis or light trace we can instruct a person to do anything. Even though that is true, the client doesn't need to know that, because they would feel uncomfortable around you, so what was said was simply giving them a deluded sense of control, when in fact they are not. It made them feel comfortable around hypnosis and therefore the session can continue.

Then I continue after the suggestibility test by saying: "Do you have any questions before you start living the life you want?"
Induce Hypnotic Trance

Dear student, remember when inducing trance within your client, you must pause when appropriate, in order to allow the client's mind to process what you are saying, and this also allows them time to respond. I am not going to write when to pause in this induction script because every induction is different, due to being personalised to the client. The feedback loop effect from observation is also important, monotone of voice and don't rush, simply talk slowly, in a relaxed manor, mirror their breathing at times, and personalise the trance from information from the pre-talk, all of which I have covered in Volume One. Continue:

As we begin you will take note of the different sounds in the room, the sound of my voice and thoughts or images that may drift through your mind and that is fine. It is now time to relax, please stare at the ceiling or light, take in a deep breath and relax as we release this breath. Continue breathing deeply and exhale slowly as you are learning to relax. As we continue here today, feeling peaceful, both you and I want to remain comfortable as you listen and concentrate on what I am saying, because what I say is important to you in achieving relaxation here today and your goal. Simply let go of all the tensions now and enjoy the feeling of being relaxed. Now you must remember, as we continue to breathe in deeply and exhale, that sometimes you can hear my voice, as you can now, and sometimes it may seem very quiet, and at times it does not matter if you cannot consciously hear my voice at all, because you cannot turn your ears off and therefore your subconscious mind will still be taking in everything that I say. You cannot turn your sense of taste, touch or smell off and you cannot turn your eyes off, you will simply closed your eyelids over them, because you cannot turn your senses off, you are always in control. Take in a deep long breath, and hold it, then in a moment breathe out, and as you do so, you are releasing all the tension from the past day, week, month and year, that you may have experienced. Now allow your head to stay where it is and start to look down, as if you are looking down at your feet, even if you cannot see them. In a moment I am going to turn on some relaxing music that is going to help you relax even more as we continue.

(Turn backing induction music on)

Allow any thoughts you may have to float into the distance, as you become more and more relaxed as time goes by. Your eyes are now becoming so tired that they simply close, and as they do, you feel even more relaxed. Allow yourself to go to (yawn so that the client can hear you because this creates sameness as if having the same experience), a sleep-like state, so that what I say will go deeper into your subconscious mind and this will prove to be one hundred percent successful for you, that feeling of relaxation is wonderful, and we both know how wonderful relaxation feels, as you drift deeper as we continue. You are going to relax into a level of relaxing that you have only ever imagined until now. The mind and body connections are very powerful and as we continue you concentrate on what I say, your mind takes in this information and your body reacts by drifting deeper and deeper into a sleep-like relaxed state. Every time you breathe in, you then breathe out all that past tension as it floats away into the distance; this guarantees your success here today. You are an intelligent person and I know this because you have understood everything that I have educated you with so far today; this also guarantees that you are able to achieve your goal from this moment forwards and you know you are now also achieving relaxation. It may happen slowly at first, each person is different and we all relax at different levels over different periods of time and that is fine. The beauty of this is that it is void of having to do anything, simply relax and let go naturally.

Deepening Trance via Staircase

Now going deeper into relaxation as we continue and you can still hear my voice, and in order to travel deeper into this wonderful sleep-like state, we are going to travel down, all the way down the staircase of relaxation within our powerful minds, this staircase consist of ten steps, see yourself right now at the top on stair ten. This staircase could be anywhere you want it to be, anywhere your imagination takes you, up in the clouds, in the park or anywhere you feel comfortable, like on the beach maybe or even in your own home, as long as you see yourself at the top, on the tenth step of the staircase of relaxation, then the location does not matter as long as you like the location. I am going to count down from ten to one, and as I do, you will imagine yourself stepping down each step with each number that I count down on the staircase of relaxation. For every step you take down, you will drift ten times deeper into relaxation, drifting deeper and deeper into a sleep-like state. And on ten, see yourself stepping, drifting, and floating down, all the way down to step nine going ten times deeper into relaxation with every step you take. Step nine drifting down with your whole body, sinking down, feeling heavier, and heavier as we step down to eight. And on eight, for every breath you breathe in and then out, you are exhaling all the past tensions as we allow you to drift deeper downwards into a sleep-like trance state. Stepping, floating down now to step seven, going ten times deeper into relaxation with every number counted down as we float downwards towards step six. And on six, every muscle in your body relaxing more, and more, getting heavier each and every time you breathe out, stepping down another step to number five. Continue to concentrate on my voice, allow yourself to let go because it feels so nice to relax more than you have for many years. And we continue to go down the staircase of relaxation to step four, feeling wonderful and enjoying this experience as it happens totally naturally, without any effort whatsoever. Step three now, see yourself floating down even further releasing all that past tension as we go, as you relax. In a moment we are going to reach the bottom of the staircase of relaxation, as we drift down to step two, and on one deeply relaxed, your whole body relaxed.

Continue by Deepening Trance Further via Bed Image

Now that we have drifted down the staircase of relaxation, and now at the bottom we can allow your body to relax even more, because I want you to imagine that there is a large comfortable double bed at the bottom of this staircase, where you are now. See yourself walking over to that warm comfortable bed, pulling the covers back and slowly climbing into that safe environment, lying down, pulling that warm blanket over you right now. And as you relax you take one last yawn,(once again yawn so that the client can hear you because this creates sameness as if having the same experience).And that sleep-like state feels warm and safe as we continue further into relaxation. Allow your mind to concentrate only on my voice at all times, as you enter that dreamlike state that feels so wonderful.

Continue by Deepening Trance Further via Body Parts

We are now ready to relax each and every area of your body, and we are going to start with your head area working downwards into relaxation. Each and every muscle in your forehead, right now relaxing, and your cheeks both cheeks relaxing, drifting down, feeling effortless as you continue to relax. Your jaw relaxing and eye lids are getting heavier and heavier, your whole face and head relaxing feeling sleepier, heavier, drifting down, and relaxing. Now moving down towards your neck area, relaxing, your head may drift to one side as you are becoming more and more tired and relaxed. Each and every muscle within your body is going deeper and deeper into a sleep-like state. You will enjoy this relaxed state as we continue, moving down, drifting down to your shoulders, both shoulders feeling limp as they relax even more, you now feel so lethargic, sinking down, feeling heavy as we move down both arms. Allowing them to go limp and drift downwards into a sleep-like state, sinking down into deep relaxation. Concentrate on your chest and stomach area, with each and every breath you breathe out you are sinking further and further down whilst enjoying the experience. Drifting down both arms, relaxing going limp and heavy towards both hands now, imagine all those muscles in each and every finger and both thumbs going limp, heavy and relaxed. (Add your observations of the client's hands and other body parts once mentioned.)

Feeling so tired and relaxed, it is so easy to achieve this relaxed state by simply allowing it to happen naturally and enjoying the relaxation as you breathe in and out relaxing more. Now from the top of your legs, as we work down to your knees achieving relaxation as you drift off feeling calm, safe, and warm. Downwards now, down both legs, relaxing down to your ankles. With every breath you take in, you then breathe out and sink even further down. Imagine your feet, allowing your toes to go limp, both feet limp, relaxed and heavy. All the way from the top of your head, all the way down to your feet, you are now deeply relaxed. And this feeling of relaxation continues as you concentrate on my voice, because what I say is very important to you, because it encourages your subconscious to remember that you are achieving relaxation, and by doing so you will also achieve your goal, for which you came here today.

Continue by Deepening Trance Further if Needed

We are now going to travel into a deeper state of relaxation from the count of ten moving down to one, and drifting ten times deeper, feeling more relaxed with every number heard being counted down. And on ten, drifting, and floating down, all the way down to a deeper state of trance. And on nine going ten times deeper into relaxation with every number being counted down, drifting down with your whole body, sinking down, feeling heavier, and heavier. And on eight, for every breath you breathe in and then out, you are exhaling all the past tensions away as you drift deeper downwards into a sleep-like trance state. Stepping, floating down now going deeper, going ten times deeper into relaxation with every number I count down, as you float downwards towards your desired goal and step seven, relaxing. And on six, every muscle in your body relaxing more and more, getting heavier with each and every breath, breathing out, drifting down towards number five. Continue to concentrate on my voice, allow yourself to let go because it feels so nice to relax more than you have for many years. We continue to count down to four, closer to the level of relaxation needed for success, feeling wonderful and enjoying this experience as it happens, totally naturally, without any effort whatsoever. Three now, I want you to see yourself floating down even further releasing all that past tension as we go, and relax. In a moment you are going to reach the desired level of relaxation as you drift down to number two, and on one deeply relaxed, your whole body relaxed.

Hypnotic Therapy Session Begins and Ends

Dear student, slightly up your tone from monotone to low volume normal speech, then continue:

As you sit, feeling drowsy and relaxed you continue to listen to my voice giving you all the positive suggestions that you require. As we continue you remain in the pleasant state of mind that you are now in. Remaining relaxed and peaceful, even drifting deeper as time goes by. Your whole body developing even further those deep, relaxing, warm feelings from the top of your head to your feet. We are now going to expand upon this new knowledge that you have required here today, making this a permanent part of your new way of thinking. The negative past will simply evaporate like a cloud on a summer's day and a new you will start to emerge for positive effect. My voice may seem to fade into the distance at times, and other times you are fully aware of what I say, this is totally normal as you drift between different levels of trance. Everything I say will seep deep into your subconscious mind, and remain there for your benefit, so that you can act upon the positive suggestions from this day forwards.

Associating Good Feeling to an Anchor

I now want to remember the memory of a time when you felt really good about yourself, we talked about this in the pre-talk when you were telling me about (use information from pre-talk and talk in an excitable positive tone), you feel really happy in that time so see yourself their now, relive it. And when you have that happy, emotional feeling from that past time, I want you to expand upon it, see the situation that you are in, and that wonderful feeling that is generated within you. The content details of the memory are not that important. What is important now for you are the emotional, happy feelings that the memory generates within you.

(Personalise from information previously given from the pre-talk.)

I want you to really remember how you felt inside, those good, positive feelings, and strong feelings, confident and self-assured feelings and the laughter from that time. You can allow those good feelings to grow stronger and more positive whilst you take in a really long, deep breath, in through your nose, and now let's associate that good feeling to pressing together your thumb and the forefinger of the right hand, and by doing so you are making the ring of confidence, so that you are associating that good feeling to making the ring of confidence with your thumb and the forefinger which becomes the anchor. This is an associated emotion to an anchor, when we experience two things together for a little while, one will automatically remind us of the other, and repetition is the mother of success, so keep repeating this exercise over the following days and weeks, so that you are making the anchor of the ring of confidence with your finger and thumb into a signal to your subconscious mind to make you feel good, because that is the happy emotion that is now associated to the ring of confidence. So whenever you take in a really long deep breath through your nose and press together your thumb and the forefinger of the right hand, you are going to feel those good, strong, confident happy feelings once again, and you can feel these good feelings anytime you wish, anywhere, in any situation. Because these good, strong, confident feelings are becoming more and more a part of you and you are becoming that stronger, more confident person that will guarantee your success in achieving your goal of overcoming (whatever the problem was). And remember, anytime you want to feel even more confident, all you need to do is breathe in that really long, deep breath through your nose and press together the thumb and the forefinger of the right hand, and you will once again feel those good, strong, confident feelings filling your whole body in order to make you feel better and better. You can feel wonderful, calmer, more relaxed and much more confident than ever before. You know what it's like to feel those good, strong, confident feelings and you can really enjoy remembering and experiencing those feelings once again, which are becoming more and more a permanent part of you. Feels good doesn't it (suggested command and not a question). Send me a sign that it feels good by raising your right hand (this was using the anchor from pre-talk triggering the right answer). Of course it does because you just created a new more positive reality for yourself, and simply relax and put your right hand down now and that's fantastic. Work on generating good feeling and then press together the thumb and the forefinger over the next few days to reinforce the anchor trigger of good feeling, and see how real that associated anchor triggers the good feeling that can be used in the future whenever you need it. Any time in the future should you have a silly thought towards a past negative problem, simply do as you just have and feel good by saying no to the silly old problem, or use the anchor when in a bad situation to make you feel good, however right now, you can relax and let go of the ring of confidence, because it is not needed at this moment in time.

Go to that Happy Place Again

I now want you to go to that happy, comfy tranquil place again within your mind, clearly see yourself there now relaxing, and I want you to put a TV screen in this happy relaxing secure place. The TV screen could be floating in front of you anywhere you like as long as you can see the screen, see the screen clearly. Showing on the screen you see a black and white paused image of yourself in a situation just before the experience in which you thought you had a phobic response towards spiders (or whatever it may be) in the past. This is the same experience in which we talked about before, so in this happy place watching this TV see a black and white paused image of yourself in the situation just before the spider experience. Now, I would like you to imagine that you float out of your body so that you can see yourself in front of you, in your happy place, looking at the TV screen. So you can see yourself sitting in your happy relaxing place looking at the black and white image of yourself on the screen. It is as if you have now become detached from yourself, so that you can see yourself sitting there now looking at that paused image on the TV screen.

Now, I want you to turn that image into a black and white movie by pressing play and watch it running all the way through that experience in which you used to have a phobic response. Let it run all the way to the end (talk the client through the experience the same as they told you in pre-talk), and pause it as a still image at the end. As you remain detached from your body, watching yourself looking at the TV screen, I now want you to watch yourself float into the TV screen and into your body, in that still image, that you have just paused. Now allow that out-of-date memory in that film to run backwards but this time in colour. Run the film backwards quickly now, faster and faster rewinding those seconds and minutes so you are watching yourself moving backwards very, very fast, all the sounds are played backwards very fast, watching yourself in that movie. All the way back to the beginning now, before anything happened. That is good. When you have done that, just remember you are in your happy place from outside of the TV screen simply watching. You are safe and secure in your happy place. At any time you can make the ring of confidence to feel even better in your happy place, so you are always in control.

Now run the movie forwards, but this time with you in the movie, so see yourself entering that TV and movie feeling confident and happy as you are now. Check how you feel dealing with that situation in which you used to experience the phobic response as you are in the movie that is now playing once again. If at any time you feel a phobic response, simply make the ring of confidence and go back to your happy place outside of the TV movie, do that now, run that old movie again (talk the client through the experience the same as they told you in pre-talk once again), then pause it once again at the end. Make the ring of confidence and come out of that movie, back into your happy place, and just relax, that's it. Good. You can do this any time you feel a phobic response, so that at all times you are in full control and safe and secure. Now, we can run the movie backwards again in just a minute. But this time, allow yourself to hear the funniest, most ludicrous background music or situation you can imagine (information from pre-talk). Something from the Muppet Show maybe. OK, now, step into that TV again and that movie and run that film backwards the same as before but with the silly music. Do that right now all the way back to the beginning. (Take whatever time is needed to do this.) Excellent, and relax. And now allow that TV screen to go blank just like that old memory and get a sense of feeling safe and secure.

Dear student, run through the movie a few times and assess the client's response, so that you can word the session accordingly. Make it humorous so that there is no sense of fear within the client's mind, in order to change the associated past emotion from fear (pain) to pleasure.
Associate Past Phobia to an object of Fun

I now want you to imagine that you are sat at home feeling safe warm and secure. You are in the living room on your own couch and you hear a small faint tap on the front door, tap, tap and tap. But you are too comfortable to get up so you shout come in and the door opens but you cannot see any one there. So you shout: "Who's there, hello." And you hear a little sob and a squeaky little voice say: "It's me, down here, it's me." You look down and in front of you see a friendly little spider sitting there crying his eyes out, he is so upset because wrapped around one of his legs, is a red hanky and his other seven legs are slipping around in his own tears. You ask the spider what's wrong and he tells you that he's lost one of his bright yellow clown shoes, and he asks you to help him find it. "Will you help me find my shoe?" Just then a huge smile comes across his face and he shouts: "There it is I can see my lost shoe, I've found it." He walks over to the missing shoe and puts it on: "Great" he says "I have all my eight shoes back." He then makes a hat with the red hanky he had on his foot before he found his missing shoe. He ties the four corners of the hanky and places it on his head. The spider looks so funny that you start to smile and laugh. The next time you see a spider you will instantly remember this little spider with yellow clown shoes and a red hanky for a hat, and you will simply smile because you now know that they are our friends, because they are harmless lovely creatures. So from this moment on you will happy to see little friendly spider because they are only saying hello. Let us now go through that movie again where you once had the reaction of a phobic response with spiders but this time with this same friendly spider in his clown shoes. (Talk the client through the situation where they once had a phobic response but this time with this funny spider). You will now find that you are totally relaxed whenever you see a spider because they are our friends. They help us get rid of the germ ridden flies. They are helping us live in a cleaner world. So from now on you are kind to spiders and kind to yourself. Just let spiders get on with their lives and you will find that you can get on with yours, feeling happy around friendly little helpless spiders.

Improve Confidence Relevant to the Session Type, via a Thermometer to 100% Successful

Now (client's name), imagine a thermometer filled with water, you know what a thermometer looks like and this one has water within it that you can see through the clear glass of the thermometer. It has the numbers one to one hundred percent written on the glass of the thermometer from the bottom to one hundred percent being at the top. This thermometer represents your confidence level from feelings in the past towards your past phobia (or low confidence etc). It may be set at ten percent at the moment; even so we need to achieve a level of one hundred percent for this session to be successful. So let's imagine heating up the water that is within the thermometer with a flame thrower. The water lever is at ten percent at the moment, making your confidence level ten percent, however by heating up the thermometer the percentage level will rise as the water heats up and therefore your confidence level will rise also. By heating up the water your confidence level starts to rise up and up, making your confidence level improve, and rapidly rising 20% 30% 40%. See the level of your confidence rise as you heat up the thermometer with the flamethrower, moving the level up higher and higher, improving your confidence level, and as it does move upwards it is getting closer to one hundred percent, you feel even more confident as the water level and confidence rises. Once the desired level of one hundred percent has been achieved, I want you to send me a sign to confirm that this confidence thermometer is at one hundred percent by raising a finger on the right hand upwards, this indicates to me that we can move on to the next part of this technique. (Wait for the signal then move on). Turn the brightness up in your mind so that you can clearly see the improved overall confidence level, and considering this thermometer is filled with water, and that water is now at one hundred percent representing your achievement made here today, it needs to remain there at one hundred percent. To do this we need to place the thermometer into the fridge freezer. See yourself now; picking up the thermometer and walking over to the freezer, opening the door and placing your confidence level of one hundred percent within the freezer, your confidence level is now frozen forever at one hundred percent and it will remain there forever because it is now frozen. Fantastic, feels good because you have achieved a lot within this session, and you have overcome your past problem, so that your new positive life can start today.

Post Hypnotic Suggestion

It is now very helpful and pleasant to go back to the good feeling anchor that we created earlier, by making the ring of confidence once again with your finger and thumb. Make the ring of confidence now, I want you to see yourself in that positive time once again, and feel how good it does now as it did back then. We have improved your overall way of thinking here today for positive effect from now and in to the continued future. You know that you can use this ring of confidence whenever you choose to, making you feel relaxed and calm around any situation that in the past you had a silly though towards. This wonderful feeling of being relaxed and comfortable is a simple state of mind that you can enter whenever you choose to, because we have proven here today that you can relax more than you have in many years. You have now placed yourself in a positive reality and that old reality has now gone forever, this is due to your new understanding of yourself and the past problem. Your goal has been achieved here today and you can now move on with your life, free from that past problem. All this new knowledge that you have learned here today has been stored within your subconscious mind, and this information can and will be used whenever you need a reminder to help you through situations that you may find yourself in. All the suggestions your subconscious mind has taken in today are for the greater good for you and the people around you. You will act upon the suggestions you have received because you now know how to succeed, and you know you have and you will continue to succeed from this day forwards. You have confronted and won your past fear hear today and you will continue to do so in the future. I am going to give you a hypnotherapy audio CD that you will take home and it will help you relax as you have here today. You will play it once every day, from today when you have a moment to yourself, or even in bed tonight and each night. Work on the good feeling anchor every day in the future for the next thirty days, so that it becomes a permanent, positive part of you.

☐

End Session by Waking the Client from Trance

Dear student, the following is said in a growing, excitable, uplifting, positive tone:

I am now going to count from one to ten, and after the count from one to ten you are going to fully awaken. This process will be slow giving you time to come around into a fully conscious state in your own time. Once fully conscious you will be so grateful and relieved that your past problem has gone. You also realise the amazing positive change within yourself, this has been a positive life changing experience for you. Previously you had not been able to relax for years but yet you have come here today to a total stranger's home, and done what you thought impossible, relaxed. What you have achieved today is amazing; in many respects it has been a revelation for you. It has been achieved by a simple change in your though processes, it is a state of mind that will now remain with you for life, for continued success.

And 1 – All the suggestions I have given you today will remain with you for life because you know how beneficial they are to you.

And 2 – From this day and every day in the future, this new beginning for you will fill you with joy of achieving your goal here today.

And 3 – Every morning you will be so happy to have this new beginning free from your past problem.

And 4 – Each day that passes you will get stronger and stronger as that past problem disappears into the distance, gone forever.

And 5 – Remembering to work on that good feeling anchor that we have created for positive effect today.

And 6 – All this new knowledge you now have, you can and will adapt it within all aspects of your life.

And 7 – Today you have been able to relax more than you have for many years, proving that you can achieve anything once you focus your mind on your goal.

And 8 – Each and every area of your body feeling refreshed and revitalised, ready to start your new way of life.

And 9 – In your own time, when you feel ready, simply open your eyes remembering all that has been said today.

And 10 – Fully awake now feeling amazing.

Dear student, Give the client a hypnotherapy relaxation CD and once again tell them they must listen to it every day, or night, as a booster to the session for at least thirty days for added support. This also helps them to work on the positive anchoring technique.

Your Journey Continues as this Book Ends

DEAR STUDENT, our journey together is close to completion. However the journey never ends, because life is a journey and not a destination, and the same can be said for your growing knowledge. If anyone ever says they know it all, about any subject, then they are very wrong, because there is always more to learn. After years of experience, it took me a further three years to write the first edition of my book: "Beginner to Advanced Practitioner Training Course & Self Development in Psychotherapy - Hypnotherapy - Neuro-Linguistic Programming (NLP) - Cognitive Behavioural Therapy (CBT) Clinical Psychology Vol: 1". Ten years later I am still adding more information, as I also continue to learn from experience, and I continue to share it with you.

I have written four script books. Those being: Phobia - Confidence & Anxiety - Weight Loss – Stop Smoking. You may want to invest in those script books as well.

You may be interested to know that I am working on a series of follow-up books to compliment my "Beginners to Advanced Volume One Book". The next book, which is the second volume, is very different than the first. Allow me to explain:

The entire client examples in all the script books, and in volume one are real, although what I have not done here, or in the first volume book, is write word for word, from beginning to the end, the dialog from full sessions of what my clients and myself have said. Instead, I wrote small sections of sessions from my experiences, to explain techniques to you and how clients think. I also wrote scripts to give you different ideas of what can be said. One of those books you have just read. The scripts were written in a way not intended to be read out to the clients word for word. I simply wanted to show you different, basic beginners and advanced ways of conducting therapy, in a structured session that you can personalise to each client.

In the next series of books starting from volume two onwards, I have written in full detail what is said from recordings that I have made of real client sessions. So the follow-up series, of books, are client case studies with each book being a different client case. In those books I will explain in detail the techniques I am using and why I have said certain things to the client, and I will explain the client's reactions. The client case study sessions were conducted at an advanced level, because that is how I conduct sessions, and therefore those books are for students that have already read volume one, and not just a scripts.

For those wishing to buy the CD's that are mentioned in this book, they are available on one CD Rom for your computer and it has eleven audio hypnotherapy Mp3's with free copyright. This allows you to make copies on CD to sell to your clients to maximise your profits and to help the clients further. They focus on: Stopping Smoking, Losing Weight, Boosting Confidence, Stress Relief, Improving Study Habits, Focus of Concentration, and Pre-talk. Also an induction backing track with subliminal messages of relaxation is on the CD, and that you can play in the back ground as you hypnotise your client.

Simply go to: www.inspiredhypnotherapy.com and then click on the: 'Prices & Online Store' page. You can also contact me through the web site if you wish to have personal training from me.

For those students that have studied this book as a Home Study Course, if you wish to take the Diploma exam, then the option to do so is available as shown on my web site: www.InspiredHypnotherapy.com on the page: "Prices & Online Store". The exam is done in your own free time from the comfort of your own home. You simply email me your answers. Students that pass will receive a Diploma Certificate, as shown on the web site.

Please add me on Facebook – 'David Glenn - Psychotherapy NLP CBT Hypnotherapy'. I am building a community of like-minded people, including my past students. I will post information on my new published books, and we can all help one another with questions and answers regarding psychotherapy as a whole.

Dear student, if you have any questions you want answering to further your knowledge, or you simply want to talk, then please phone me. Phone calls are free via Wi-Fi on WhatsApp from anywhere in the World. Telephone 07973481786

Of course I have to charge for my time. Those charges being £25 for half hour or less. Or £45 for over half an hour to an hour. We can cover many topics in that time. Payment must be made online before the call is made in order to schedule a time and date for our conversation.

I also conduct therapy sessions over the phone if you, or someone you know can't travel to see me in person at the same cost.

Simply email me your details, how much of my time you wish to have, dates and UK times that you are free to talk, and I shall email you a request for payment and set scheduled session. Alternatively in person I charge £95 for a full one and a half hour session.

david.glenn.psychotherapy@gmail.com

Dear student. Can I please ask for a few moments of your time to leave positive feedback on the site where you invested in this book? Without feedback, my time writing will have been wasted, because few people will invest in the book and I simply want to help people to study, to help others, and also for people to overcome their personal psychological problems.

Please note that I am not a professional writer. I am a therapist. Even so, I have done my best to write this book to help others and you. So please excuse the odd grammar error or spelling mistake. This book has been written in UK English and not American-English and for that reason many words are spelt differently to what our American friends are used to.

Thank you!

Dear student, I wish you all the happiness in the world and good health, until our paths cross again in 'Volume One or Two or more' or another script book. Bye for now.